ELVIS AND ME

"This honest, full-length portrait paints him as he really was both in and out of the spotlight...his wife, who knew him better than anyone else, sees him clearly, steadily, and sees him whole."

—*John Barkham Reviews*

"Her love for him...jumps out from between the lines."
—Marilyn Beck, New York *Daily News*

"A sad, sweet book...the story it tells is fascinating."
—*Washington Post*

"A love story unlike any other...warm, dramatic and vivid...full of heartbreak as well as tender feelings...the author ingeniously weaves a tapestry of emotions...a must for all Elvis fans and friends."

—*The Waco Citizen*

"ELVIS AND ME is one fast and titillating read."
—*Daily News*

ELVIS
AND
ME

Priscilla Beaulieu Presley
with Sandra Harmon

BERKLEY BOOKS, NEW YORK

This Berkley book contains the complete
text of the original hardcover edition.

ELVIS AND ME

A Berkley Book / published by arrangement with
G. P. Putnam's Sons

PRINTING HISTORY
G. P. Putnam's edition / September 1985
Berkley edition / August 1986

ISBN: 0-425-09103-1

A BERKLEY BOOK ® TM 757,375
Berkley Books are published by The Berkley Publishing Group,
200 Madison Avenue, New York, NY 10016.
The name "BERKLEY" and the "B" logo
are trademarks belonging to Berkley Publishing Corporation.

PRINTED IN THE UNITED STATES OF AMERICA

20 19 18 17 16 15 14

ACKNOWLEDGMENTS

Without them this book could not have been possible. I am forever grateful and want to thank:

Michelle and Gary Hovey for the love and sensitivity you shared and for the countless hours of "being there for me."

My Mother and Father: I regret I have only this lifetime to return all the love and understanding you gave me.

Jerry Schilling, my true friend, whom I've always been able to count on.

Joe Esposito, for always being dependable.

Joel Stevens: I couldn't have made it without you, my friend!

Ellis Amburn, for his patience and dedication.

Norman Brokaw and Owen Laster, for their constant belief in me.

Also, for their invaluable contributions:
Sandy Harmon
Steven Kral
Phyllis Grann

For Lisa Marie

"Don't criticize what you don't understand, son, you never walked in that man's shoes."

ELVIS AARON PRESLEY

1

IT WAS August 16, 1977, overcast and dreary, not a typical Southern California day. When I walked outside, there was a stillness, an unnatural calm in the air that I have not experienced since. I almost went back into the house, unable to shake my uneasiness. I had a meeting that morning and by noon I was racing to meet my sister Michelle. On my way into Hollywood I noticed the atmosphere had not changed. It still seemed unusually silent and depressing and it had begun to drizzle. As I drove down Melrose Avenue, I saw Michelle standing on the corner, a look of concern on her face. "Cilla, I just got a call from Dad," she said as I pulled up. "Joe's been trying to reach you. It's something about Elvis in the hospital." Joe Esposito was Elvis's road manager and right-hand man. I froze. If he was trying to reach me, something must be terribly wrong. I told Michelle to take her car and quickly follow me home.

I made a U-turn in the middle of the street and raced back to the house like a madwoman. Every conceivable possibility went through my mind. Elvis had been in and out of the hospital all year; there were times when he wasn't even sick that he'd check in for a rest, to get away from pressures, or just out of boredom. It had never been anything too serious.

I thought about our daughter, Lisa, who was visiting Elvis at Graceland and was supposed to come home that very day. Oh God, I prayed. Please let everything be all right. Don't let anything happen, please, dear God.

I ran every red light and nearly hit a dozen cars. At last, I reached home, and as I swerved down the driveway, I could hear the phone ringing from inside the house. Please don't hang up, I prayed, jumping out of the car and running toward the door. "I'm coming," I yelled. I tried to get my key in the lock, but my hand wouldn't stop shaking.

Finally I got into the house, grabbed the receiver, and yelled, "Hello, hello?"

All I could hear was the hum of a long-distance line, then a stricken, faint voice, "Cilla. It's Joe."

"What's happened, Joe?"

"It's Elvis."

"Oh, my God. Don't tell me."

"Cilla, he's dead."

"Joe, don't tell me that. Please!"

"We've lost him."

"No. NO!" I begged him to take back his words. Instead, he was silent. "We've lost him—" His voice broke and we both began to cry. "Joe, where's Lisa?" I asked.

"She's okay. She's with Grandma."

"Thank God. Joe, send a plane for me, please. And hurry. I want to come home."

As I hung up, Michelle and Mother, who had just arrived, embraced me and we cried in each other's arms. Within minutes the phone rang again. For a moment I hoped for a miracle; they were calling me back to tell me that Elvis was still alive, that it was all right, that it had all been a bad dream.

But there were no miracles. "Mommy, Mommy," Lisa was saying. "Something's happened to Daddy."

"I know, Baby," I whispered. "I'll be there soon. I'm waiting for the plane now."

"Everybody's crying, Mommy."

I felt helpless. What could I say to her? I couldn't even find words to comfort myself. I feared what she would be hearing. She didn't yet know that he had died. All I kept saying over and over was, "I'll be there as soon as I can. Try to stay in Grandma's room, away from everyone." In the background I could hear a grief-stricken Vernon moaning in agony. "My son's gone. Dear God, I've lost my son."

Fortunately a child's innocence provides its own protection. Death was not yet a reality to her. She said she'd go out and play with Laura, her friend.

I hung up and walked around in a daze, still numb with shock. The news hit the media instantly. My phones did not stop ringing, with friends trying to cope with the shock, members of the family grasping for explanations, and the press demanding statements. I locked myself in the bedroom and left instructions that I would not speak to anyone, that I wanted to be alone.

In fact, I wanted to die. Love is very deceiving. Though we were divorced, Elvis was still an essential part of my life. Over the last years we'd become good friends, admitting the mistakes we'd made in the past and just beginning to laugh at our shortcomings. I could not face the reality that I would never see him alive again. He had always been there for me. I depended on him, just as he depended on me. We had a bond: We'd become closer and had more understanding and patience for each other than in our married life. We had even talked of one day . . . And now he was gone.

I remembered our last phone conversation, just a few days before. His mood had been good as he talked about the twelve-day tour he was about to begin. He even laughed when he told me that, as usual, the Colonel had papered the first city they were scheduled to hit with his posters and that his records were being played constantly in advance of his arrival.

"Good old Colonel," Elvis had said. "We've come a long way. He's still puttin' out that same old stuff. It's a wonder people are still buying it."

I loved hearing Elvis laugh, something he had been doing less and less. Just days before that last call, I'd heard that his spirits were down and he was contemplating breaking up with Ginger Alden, his girlfriend. I knew him well enough to realize that this was not an easy move for him to make. If only I'd known that would be the last time I'd talk to him, I'd have said so much more: things I wanted to say and never had, things I'd held inside me for so many years because the timing was always wrong.

He had been a part of my life for eighteen years. When we met, I had just turned fourteen. The first six months I spent with him were filled with tenderness and affection. Blinded by love, I saw none of his faults or weaknesses. He was to become the passion of my life.

He taught me everything: how to dress, how to walk, how to apply makeup and wear my hair, how to behave, how to return love—his way. Over the years he became my father, husband, and very nearly God. Now he was gone and I felt more alone and afraid than ever in my life.

The hours went by slowly before Elvis's private plane, the *Lisa Marie*, arrived. Behind closed doors I sat and waited, remembering our life together—the joy, the pain, the sadness, and the triumphs—from the very first time I heard his name.

2

IT WAS 1956. I was living with my family at the Bergstrom Air Force Base in Austin, Texas, where my father, then Captain Joseph Paul Beaulieu, a career officer, was stationed. He came home late for dinner one evening and handed me a record album.

"I don't know what this Elvis guy is all about," he said, "but he must be something special. I stood in line with half the Air Force at the PX to get this for you; everybody wants it."

I put the record on the hi-fi and heard the rocking music of "Blue Suede Shoes." The album was titled *Elvis Presley*. It was his first.

Like almost every other kid in America, I liked Elvis but not as fanatically as many of my girlfriends at Del

Valley Junior High. They all had Elvis T-shirts and Elvis hats and Elvis bobby sox and even lipstick in colors with names like Hound Dog Orange and Heartbreak Pink. Elvis was everywhere, on bubble-gum cards and Bermuda shorts, on diaries and wallets and pictures that glowed in the dark. The boys at school began trying to look like him, with their slicked-back pompadours and long sideburns and turned-up collars.

One girl was so crazy about him that she was running his local fan club. She said I could join for twenty-five cents, the price of a book she'd ordered for me by mail. When I received it, I was shocked to see a picture of Elvis signing the bare chests of a couple of girls, at that time an unheard-of act.

Then I saw him on television on Jimmy and Tommy Dorsey's *Stage Show*. He was sexy and handsome, with his deep brooding eyes, pouty lips, and crooked smile. He strutted out to the microphone, spread his legs, leaned back, and strummed his guitar. Then he began singing with such confidence, moving his body with un-bridled sexuality. Despite myself, I was attracted.

Some members of his adult audience were less enthu-siastic. Soon his performances were labeled obscene. My mother stated emphatically that he was "a bad influence for teenage girls. He arouses things in them that shouldn't be aroused. If there's ever a mothers' march against Elvis Presley, I'll be the first in line."

But I'd heard that despite all of his stage antics and lustful, tough-guy looks, Elvis came from a strict South-ern Christian background. He was a country boy who didn't smoke or drink, who loved and honored his parents, and who addressed all adults as "sir" or "ma'am."

I was an Air Force child, a shy, pretty little girl, unhappily accustomed to moving from base to base every two or three years. By the time I was eleven, I had lived in six different cities and, fearful of not being accepted, I either kept to myself or waited for someone to befriend me. I found it especially difficult entering a new school in the middle of the year, when cliques had already been established and newcomers were considered outsiders.

Small and petite, with long brown hair, blue eyes, and an upturned nose, I was always stared at by the other students. At first girls would see me as a rival, afraid I'd take their boyfriends away. I seemed to feel more comfortable with boys—and they were usually friendlier.

People always said I was the prettiest girl in school, but I never felt that way. I was skinny, practically scrawny, and even if I was as cute as people said, I wanted to have more than just good looks. Only with my family did I really feel totally protected and loved. Close and supportive, they provided my stability.

A photographer's model before her marriage, my mother was totally devoted to her family. As the oldest, it was my responsibility to help her with the kids. After me, there were Don, four years my junior, and Michelle, my only sister, who was five years younger than Don. Jeff and the twins, Tim and Tom, hadn't yet been born.

My mother was too shy to talk about the facts of life, so my sex education came in school, when I was in the sixth grade. Some kids were passing around a book that looked like the Bible from the outside, but when you opened it, there were pictures of men making love to women, and women making love to each other.

My body was changing and stirring with new feelings. I'd gotten looks from boys at school, and once a picture of me in a tight turtleneck sweater was stolen from the school bulletin board. Yet I was still a child, embarrassed about my own sexuality. I fantasized endlessly about French-kissing, but when my friends who hung around our house played spin the bottle, it would take me half an hour to let a boy kiss my pursed lips.

My strong, handsome father was the center of our world. He was a hard worker who had earned his degree in Business Administration at University of Texas. At home he ran a tight ship. He was a firm believer in discipline and responsibility, and he and I frequently knocked heads. When I became a cheerleader at thirteen, it was all I could do to convince him to let me go to out-of-town games. Other times no amount of crying, pleading, or appealing to my mother would change his mind. When he laid down the law, that was that.

I managed to get around him occasionally. When he refused to let me wear a tight skirt, I joined the Girl Scouts specifically so I could wear their tight uniform.

My parents were survivors. Although they often had to struggle financially, we children were the last to feel it. When I was a little girl my mother sewed pretty table-cloths to cover the orange crates that we used as end tables. Rather than do without, we made the best of what we had.

Dinner was strictly group participation: Mother cooked, one of us set the table, and the rest cleaned up. Nobody got away with anything, but we were very supportive of one another. I felt fortunate to have a close-knit family.

Going through old albums of family photographs showing my parents when they were young fascinated me. I was curious about the past. World War II intrigued me, especially since my father had fought with the Marines on Okinawa. He looked handsome in his uniform—you could tell he was posing for my mother—but somehow his smile looked out of place, especially when you realized where he was. When I read the note on the back of the picture about how much he missed my mother, my eyes filled with tears.

While rummaging through the family keepsakes I came upon a small wooden box. Inside was a carefully folded American flag, the kind that I knew was given to servicemen's widows. Also inside the box was a picture of my mother with her arm around a strange man and, sitting on her lap, an infant. On the back of the photo was inscribed "Mommy, Daddy, Priscilla." I had discovered a family secret.

Feeling betrayed, I ran to phone my mother, who was at a party nearby. Within minutes I was in her arms, crying as she calmed me and explained that when I was six months old, my real father, Lieutenant James

Wagner, a handsome Navy pilot, had been killed in a plane crash while returning home on leave. Two and a half years later, she married Paul Beaulieu, who adopted me and had always loved me as his own.

Mother suggested I keep my discovery from the other children. She felt it would endanger our family closeness, though when it did become known, it had no effect on our feelings for one another. She gave me a gold locket that my father had given her. I cherished that locket and wore it for years and fantasized that my father died a great hero. In times of emotional pain and loneliness he would become my guardian angel.

By the end of the year, I'd been nominated to run for Queen of Del Valley Junior High. This was my first taste of politics and competition and it was especially trying because I was running against Pam Rutherford, my best friend.

We each had a campaign manager introducing us as we went from house to house knocking on doors. My manager tried to talk each person into voting for me and donating a penny or more per vote to a school fund. The nominee who collected the most money won. I was sure that this competition would jeopardize my friendship with Pam, which was more important to me than winning. I considered quitting but felt I couldn't let my parents or my supporters down. While my mother was out looking for a dress for me to wear to the coronation, my dad kept reminding me to memorize an acceptance speech. I kept putting it off, certain I was going to lose.

It was the last day of the campaign, and a rumor began circulating that Pam's grandparents had put in a hundred-dollar bill for their vote. My parents were disappointed; there was no way that they could afford to match that much money and even if they could, they objected on principle.

The night they announced the winner, I was all dressed up in a new turquoise blue, strapless tulle net formal that itched so badly I couldn't wait to take it off. I sat beside Pam on the dais in the large school auditorium. I could see my parents with happy, confident looks on their faces though I was sure they were going to be disheartened. Then the principal walked up to the podium.

"And now," she said, hesitating to heighten the suspense, "is the moment you've all been waiting for . . . the culmination of a month of campaigning by our two lovely contestants: Priscilla Beaulieu . . ." All eyes turned toward me. I blushed and glanced at Pam. ". . . and Pam Rutherford." Our eyes locked for a brief, tense moment.

"The new Queen of Del Valley Junior High is . . ." A drum roll sounded. ". . . Priscilla Beaulieu."

The audience applauded wildly. I was in shock. Called up to the stage to give my speech, I had none. Sure that I was going to lose, I'd never even bothered to write one. I walked, trembling, to the podium, then looked out at the crowded auditorium. All I could see was my father's face, growing more disappointed as he realized I had nothing to say. When I finally spoke, it was to apologize.

"Ladies and gentlemen, I'm sorry," I whispered. "I'm not prepared to give a speech, as I did not expect to win. But thank you very much for voting for me. I'll do my very best." And then, looking at my father, I added, "I'm sorry, Dad."

I was surprised as the audience graciously applauded, but I still had to face my father and hear him say, "I told you so."

Being elected Queen was a bittersweet victory, because the closeness that Pam and I once shared was restrained. Still, to me that crown symbolized a wonderful, unfamiliar feeling: acceptance.

My newfound tranquility ended abruptly when my father announced that he was being transferred to Wiesbaden, West Germany.

I was crushed. Germany was the other side of the world. All my fears returned. My first thought was, What am I going to do about my friends? I turned to my mother, who was sympathetic and reminded me that we were in the Air Force and moving was an unavoidable part of our lives.

I finished junior high school, my mother gave birth to baby Jeff, and we said our goodbyes to neighbors and good friends. Everyone promised to write or call, but remembering past promises I knew better. My friend Angela jokingly told me that Elvis Presley was stationed in Bad Neuheim, West Germany. "Do you believe it? You're going to be in the same country as Elvis Presley," she said. We looked at a map and found that Bad Neuheim was close to Wiesbaden. I said back, "I'm going over there to meet Elvis." We both laughed, hugged each other, and said goodbye.

The fifteen-hour flight to West Germany seemed interminable, but finally we arrived in the beautiful old city of Wiesbaden, headquarters of the U.S. Air Force in Europe. There we checked into the Helene Hotel, a massive and venerable building on the main thoroughfare. After three months, hotel living became too expensive and we began looking for a place to rent.

We felt lucky to find a large apartment in a vintage building constructed long before World War I. Soon after we moved in, we noticed that all the other apartments were rented to single girls. These *Fräuleins* walked around all day long in robes and negligees, and at night they were dressed to kill. Once we learned a little German, we realized that, although the pension was very discreet, we were living in a bordello.

Moving was out of the question—housing was too scarce—but the location did little to help me to adjust. Not only was I isolated from other American families, but there was the language barrier. I was accustomed to changing schools frequently, but a foreign country posed altogether new problems—principally that I couldn't share my thoughts. I began to feel that my life had stopped dead in its tracks.

September came and with it, school. Once again I was the new girl. I was no longer popular and secure as I'd been at Del.

There was a place called the Eagles Club, where American service families went for dinner and entertainment. It was within walking distance of the pension and soon proved an important discovery for me. Every day after school, I'd go to the snack bar there and listen to the jukebox and write letters to my friends back home in Austin, telling them how much I missed them. Drowning in tears, I'd spend my weekly allowance playing the songs that were very popular back in the States—Frankie Avalon's "Venus" and the Everly Brothers' "All I Have to Do Is Dream."

One warm summer afternoon, I was sitting with my brother Don when I noticed a handsome man in his twenties staring at me. I'd seen him watching me before, but I'd never paid any attention to him. This time, he stood up and walked toward me. He introduced himself as Currie Grant and asked my name.

"Priscilla Beaulieu," I said, immediately suspicious; he was much older than I.

He asked where in the States I came from, how I liked Germany, and if I liked Elvis Presley.

"Of course," I said, laughing. "Who doesn't?"

"I'm a good friend of his. My wife and I go to his house quite often. How would you like to join us one evening?"

Unprepared for such an extraordinary invitation, I grew even more skeptical and guarded. I told him I'd have to ask my parents. Over the course of the next two weeks, Currie met my parents and my father checked out his credentials. Currie was also in the Air Force and it turned out that my father knew his commanding officer. That seemed to break the ice between them. Currie assured Dad that I'd be well chaperoned when we visited Elvis, who lived off base in a house in Bad Nauheim.

On the appointed night I tore through my closet, trying to find an appropriate outfit. Nothing seemed dressy enough for meeting Elvis Presley. I settled on a navy and white sailor dress and white socks and shoes. Surveying myself in the mirror, I thought I looked cute, but being only fourteen, I didn't think I'd make any kind of impression on Elvis.

Eight o'clock finally arrived, and so did Currie Grant and his attractive wife, Carole. Anxious, I hardly spoke to either of them during the forty-five-minute drive. We entered the small town of Bad Nauheim, with its narrow cobblestone streets and plain, old-fashioned houses, and I kept looking around for what I assumed would be Elvis's huge mansion. Instead Currie pulled up to an ordinary-looking three-story house surrounded by a white picket fence.

There was a sign on the gate in German, which translated as: AUTOGRAPHS BETWEEN 7:00 AND 8:00 P.M. *only*. Even though it was after eight o'clock, a large group of friendly German girls waited around expectantly. When I asked Currie about them, he explained that there were always large groups of fans outside the house, hoping to catch a glimpse of Elvis.

I followed Currie through the gate and up the short pathway to the door. We were welcomed by Vernon Presley, Elvis's father, a tall, gray-haired, attractive man, who led us down a long hallway to the living room, from which I could hear Brenda Lee on the record player, singing "Sweet Nothin's."

The plain, almost drab living room was filled with people, but I spotted Elvis immediately. He was handsomer than he appeared in films, younger and more vulnerable-looking with his GI haircut. He was in civilian clothes, a bright red sweater and tan slacks, and he was sitting with one leg swung over the arm of a large over-stuffed chair, with a cigar dangling from his lips.

As Currie led me over to him, Elvis stood up and smiled. "Well," he said. "What have we here?"

I didn't say anything. I couldn't. I just kept staring at him.

"Elvis," Currie said, "this is Priscilla Beaulieu. The girl I told you about."

We shook hands and he said, "Hi, I'm Elvis Presley," but then there was a silence between us until Elvis asked me to sit down beside him, and Currie drifted off.

"So," Elvis said. "Do you go to school?"

"Yes."

"What are you, about a junior or senior in high school?"

I blushed and said nothing, not willing to reveal that I was only in the ninth grade.

"Well," he persisted.

"Ninth."

Elvis looked confused. "Ninth what?"

"Grade," I whispered.

"Ninth *grade*," he said and started laughing. "Why, you're just a baby."

"Thanks," I said curtly. Not even Elvis Presley had the right to say that to me.

"Well. Seems the little girl has spunk," he said, laughing again, amused by my response. He gave me that charming smile of his, and all my resentment just melted away.

We made small talk for a while longer. Then Elvis got

up and walked over to the piano and sat down. The room suddenly grew silent. Everyone's eyes were riveted on him as he began to entertain us.

He sang "Rags to Riches" and "Are You Lonesome Tonight?" and then with his friends singing harmony, "End of the Rainbow." He also did a Jerry Lee Lewis impersonation, pounding the keys so hard that a glass of water he'd set on the piano began sliding off. When Elvis caught it without missing a beat of the song, everyone laughed and applauded—except me. I was nervous. I glanced around the room and saw an intimidating life-size poster of a half-nude Brigitte Bardot on the wall. She was the last person I wanted to see, with her fulsome body, pouting lips, and wild mane of tousled hair. Imagining Elvis's taste in women, I felt very young and out of place.

I glanced up and saw Elvis trying to get my attention. I noticed that the less response I showed, the more he began singing just for me. I couldn't believe that Elvis Presley was trying to impress me.

Later, he asked me to come into the kitchen, where he introduced me to his grandmother, Minnie Mae Presley, who stood by the stove, frying a huge pan of bacon. As we sat down at the table, I told Elvis I wasn't hungry. Actually I was too nervous to eat.

"You're the first girl I've met from the States in a long time," Elvis said, as he began devouring the first of five gigantic bacon sandwiches, each one smothered with mustard. "Who are the kids listening to?"

I laughed. "Are you kidding?" I said. "Everyone listens to you."

Elvis seemed unconvinced. He asked me a lot of questions about Fabian and Ricky Nelson. He told me he was worried about how his fans would accept him when he returned to the States. Since he'd been away, he hadn't made any public appearances or movies, although he'd had five hit singles, all recorded before he'd left.

It felt like we'd just begun talking when Currie came in and pointed to his watch. I had dreaded that moment; the evening had gone so fast. It seemed I had just arrived and now I was being hurried away. Elvis and I had just started to get to know each other. I felt like Cinderella, knowing that when my curfew came, all this magic would end. I was surprised when Elvis asked Currie if I could possibly stay longer. When Currie explained the agreement with my father, Elvis casually suggested that maybe I could come by again. Though I wanted to more than anything in the world, I didn't really believe it would happen.

The fog was so thick on the Autobahn back to Wiesbaden that I didn't get home until 2 A.M. My parents had waited up, wanting to know everything that had happened. I told them Elvis was a gentleman, that he was funny and entertained his friends all night, and that I'd had a wonderful time.

The next day in school, I couldn't concentrate. My thoughts were entirely on Elvis. I tried to recall every word he'd said to me, every song he'd sung, every look in his eyes as he'd gazed at me. I went over and over our conversation. His charm was captivating. I told no one. Who would ever believe that just the night before, I'd been with Elvis Presley?

I never expected to hear from him again. Then, a few days later, the phone rang. It was Currie. He said he'd just got a call from Elvis, who wondered if it was possible for Currie to bring me over that night. I was ecstatic. "Currie, you don't mean it? He wants to see me? Why? When did he call?" Unable to answer all my questions, Currie said calmly, "You want me to ask your father?"

My parents were as surprised as I. They reluctantly acceded to Currie's request.

The next visit was very much like the one before—small talk, singing, Elvis playing the piano, and everyone eating Grandma's favorite dishes. But later, when Elvis had finished singing, he came up to me. "I want to be alone with you, Priscilla."

We were standing face to face, staring into each other's eyes. I looked around. The room was empty.

"We are alone," I replied nervously.

He moved closer, backing me against the wall. "I mean *really* alone," he whispered. "Will you come upstairs to my room?"

The question threw me into a panic. *His room?*

Until that moment, it hadn't crossed my mind that Elvis Presley might be interested in me sexually. He could have any girl in the world. Why would he want me?

"There's nothing to be frightened of, Honey."

As he spoke, he was smoothing my hair. "I swear I'll never do anything to harm you." He sounded absolutely sincere. "I'll treat you just like a sister." Flustered and confused, I looked away.

"Please."

Standing there looking into his eyes, I was drawn to him almost against my will. I believed him; it wasn't a difficult thing to do. I had discovered by now his intentions were warm and sincere. Moments went by and I still couldn't do anything. Then I nodded. "All right, I'll go."

He took my hand and led me toward the stairs, whispering which room was his, and said, "You go on ahead, and I'll join you in a few minutes. It looks better."

He headed toward the kitchen as I slowly climbed the stairs, wondering, What would he demand of me? Expect of me? I will be completely alone with him for the first time. Since meeting him I had dreamed of this moment, sure that it would never arrive, and now I was in the midst of a reality I'd never expected.

I reached the second floor and found his bedroom. It was as plain and impersonal as the other rooms of the house. I went in and sat down primly on a stiff-backed chair—and waited. When Elvis didn't show up after a few minutes, I began to look around. It was an ordinary room with nothing unusual, certainly nothing to imply that it belonged to a famous rock-and-roll singer. There were books, a collection of records, his uniforms, and his boots. There were several letters from girls in the States on his night table. Many were from someone named Anita. Elvis rarely mentioned Anita, but everyone knew he had a girl back home. I wanted to read the letters but was afraid he'd catch me.

It was another twenty minutes before he finally appeared. He came in, removed his jacket, turned on the radio, and then sat down on his bed. I hardly looked at him, petrified of what he might expect. I imagined him grabbing me, throwing me down on the bed, and making love to me.

Instead he said, "Why don't you come over here and sit next to me?" I was reluctant, but he assured me that I had nothing to be afraid of. "I really like you, Priscilla. You're refreshing. It's nice to talk to someone from back home. I miss that. It gets a little lonely here."

I sat next to him, saying nothing, but I was touched by his vulnerable, boyish quality. He went on to say that our relationship was going to be important to him and that he needed me. It was October and he was scheduled to return to the States in six months. He knew lots of girls, he said, and many had come to visit as I had, but I was the first girl with whom he felt a real closeness.

I cuddled into his arms, certain he would not move too fast. He held me closely, saying, "I just wish Mama could have been here to meet you." He sighed and a troubled look came over his face. "She would have liked you as much as I do."

"I wish I could have met her," I whispered, moved by his sincerity.

I was to learn that Elvis's mother, Gladys, was the love of his life. She had died on August 14, 1958, at age forty-two, of heart failure following a long siege of acute hepatitis.

He expressed how deeply he loved and missed her and how in many ways he dreaded returning to Graceland without her there. It had been his gift to her, a private estate that he'd purchased for $100,000 a year before she died.

Elvis believed that his mother had eventually given up on life. Her health had begun to deteriorate when he was drafted. Her love for Vernon and Elvis was so great that she could never face the loss of either of them and often said she wanted to be the first to go. In Gladys's naive, country way she assumed that Germany still represented war and danger. She could never comprehend that peacetime conditions now prevailed.

It was Elvis's habit to phone Gladys every day. I was surprised to learn that up until the time he began entertaining, he never spent a night away from home. He told me of the time his car caught on fire while on the road and he barely escaped with his life. Although she was miles away, Gladys sat straight up in her bed and screamed his name—the intuitive link between them was that strong. Her concern for his welfare while he was away from home was so great that she would spend sleepless nights until his call came, telling her he was safe.

When he was in basic training at Fort Hood, Texas, he rented a house off base for Vernon, Gladys, and Grandma. I felt that her death affected him more than anyone could fully understand. He blamed himself for not being with her when she fell ill and had to be sent back home to Memphis under a doctor's care.

In time he realized that Gladys had resorted to drinking, and he was very concerned that this could become a problem. As much as he consoled her, assured her that he would return in eighteen months, and even begged her to join him, Gladys's fear of losing her only son drove her to her grave.

Elvis's unrelieved depression over Gladys's death was intensified by the conflict in Elvis's mind over Dee Stanley, whom Vernon had met in Germany. Dee and his father had become inseparable shortly after Gladys's death, too soon to Elvis's liking. An attractive blonde in her thirties, Dee was in the process of divorcing her husband and was separated from him and her three children when she started dating Vernon. The thought that his father could ever conceive of replacing Gladys upset Elvis terribly. He also had doubts about Dee's intentions and whether they were in his father's best interest.

"What's Dee trying to do?" Elvis sometimes asked suspiciously. "Make him into some dude he's not? Why can't she just accept him the way he is? I've never seen him so lovesick. She meets him at some restaurant and exchanges love notes all day."

My heart went out to Elvis that night as he confided his problems and worries. He was a world-famous entertainer, a great star, and yet a terribly lonely man.

Again our visit seemed to end too soon. He kissed me goodbye, my first real kiss. I had never experienced such a mixture of affection and desire. I was speechless but closely tied to the reality of where I was—locked in his arms, my mouth against his. Aware of my response—and my youth—he broke away first, saying, "We have plenty of time, Little One." He kissed my forehead and sent me home.

By our fourth date, Dad had laid down the law: "If you want to continue seeing Elvis, we're going to have to meet him." My parents weren't so enthralled with his celebrity status that they were willing to compromise their principles. In the beginning it was convenient for Currie to come for me and bring me home, but by now my parents were asking why Elvis didn't do this himself. One Saturday night I said to Elvis, "My parents want to meet you. They want you to pick me up."

He bristled. "What do you mean?"

"I mean," I said nervously, "I can't come see you anymore unless you come and meet my parents."

He agreed—provided he could bring his father along.

That day I went through my usual routine except instead of being ready one hour in advance it was two. I waited by the window, looking for his car as I played his records—"Old Shep," "I Was the One," and "I Want You, I Need You, I Love You"—nonstop until my father yelled from the kitchen, "Do you have to play those records now? My God, the man will be here in a few minutes and you see him practically every night. I'd think you'd want to take a breather from each other."

I was nervous. I knew that Dad wanted Elvis to both pick me up and bring me home himself—and he planned to tell Elvis this.

I didn't know how Dad was going to approach him—whether he planned to be friendly or stern—and I knew only too well how stern Dad could be. I sat there, anticipating the worst.

About an hour later, I spotted Elvis's BMW and saw Elvis and his father emerge from the car. Elvis had come totally prepared; he was wearing his uniform to impress Dad. He knew that the service was their connection, and he played on it. He looked great.

He took off his hat and kissed me on the cheek. I asked

him and his father in and led them into our living room, where Elvis fidgeted and seemed, for once, at a loss for words. "Are your parents here?" he ventured. I could manage only a nod and he continued, "I know we're a little late, but I had to get cleaned up—and we had some trouble finding the place." I was amused—imagine, Elvis Presley making up excuses. I was now sufficiently aware of his habits to know that it took him three hours to change, chat with the boys, enjoy one of Grandma's huge meals, and sign a few autographs along the way. Except when he was working, he had a cavalier attitude toward time.

While Vernon settled on the couch, Elvis pointed to our family portraits on the wall and said, "Look here, Daddy—here's Priscilla with her whole family. I think she looks like her mama. Can't see too much resemblance with her brothers or sister—they're still a little too young. Don't cut your hair, Baby. I love it long like this. You're one pretty girl. How'd I happen to run into you? Must be fate." The last few observations were uttered in a whisper to me as my parents came in.

Instead of saying, "Hi," as most young men would have done, Elvis put out his hand and said, "Hello, I'm Elvis Presley and this is my daddy, Vernon."

It sounded silly to me, they knew who he was, as did the whole world. But Elvis was the perfect gentleman. My father was visibly impressed, and from that moment on, Elvis always addressed him as Captain Beaulieu or Sir. This was characteristic of Elvis, whatever a person's position in life—whether doctor or lawyer, professor or motion-picture director—unless someone were in Elvis's immediate circle, Elvis rarely used first names, even in dealing with people he'd known for years. As he once explained to me, "It's simple. They've worked hard to get where they are. Someone should respect them."

The conversation with my parents that night was just small talk. Elvis said that he'd spent a busy day at the *Kaserne* and this led to an exchange about the service.

"What did they assign you to over here?" Dad asked, implying that it had better be a solid job if Elvis wanted to take out his daughter.

"Sir, right now I'm basically driving a jeep for the Fourth Armored Division in Bad Nauheim."

"That can be tough this time of year."

"You're not kidding, sir. We've had some pretty cold nights out there already. I have to be especially careful. I battle tonsillitis when my resistance gets low, which isn't good for my voice."

"I guess you're looking forward to going home."

"Yes, sir. Only five more months."

Then Elvis asked my parents how they liked being stationed in Germany.

"Very much," Dad said. "We plan on being here for three years."

There was a sudden silence. Then Dad offered dinner, but Elvis said they didn't have time. I sat attentively, observing Elvis's uneasiness and remembering his relaxed manner in his own home. He was on his best behavior and it was endearing. Mother was reserving judgment about this rock-and-roll star she had professed to dislike so much. I could see that his Southern charm was winning her over.

Finally, my father got around to explaining to Elvis the Beaulieu dating rules. If he wanted to see me, Elvis had to pick me up and bring me home. Elvis explained that by the time he got off duty, went home, cleaned up, came to Wiesbaden and back, the evening would be gone. Would it be all right if his father would collect me?

Dad mulled this over, then expressed his concern. "Just what is the intent here? Let's face it: You're Elvis Presley. You have women throwing themselves at you. Why my daughter?"

Both Elvis and Vernon were caught off-guard. Vernon shifted from one side of the chair to the other, probably thinking, Okay, Elvis, how are you going to get out of this one?

Elvis said, "Well, sir, I happen to be very fond of her. She's a lot more mature than her age and I enjoy her company. It hasn't been easy for me, being away from home and all. It gets kinda lonely. I guess you might say I need someone to talk to. You don't have to worry about her, Captain. I'll take good care of her."

Elvis's honesty disarmed Dad, just as it did my mother. I joined Elvis as he stood, picked up his hat, and added, "Well, sir, we've got a long drive."

There was one stipulation: Elvis himself had to bring me home. He agreed, reassuring them that I would be well taken care of, that there were a lot of family members at his house. He could have ridiculed Dad's request, yet he agreed to take me home every night. I was thrilled but contained my excitement. He *really* wanted to be with me.

The next night, when Elvis brought me home, we

parked in front of the pension. He poured out his heart to me, as he would continue to do throughout our time in Germany. He was lonely. He was unsure of how he would be received by his fans when he returned to the States.

When he'd entered the Army, he had been at the pinnacle of his fame. He'd recorded seventeen straight million-selling singles and had starred in four films, all of which had become box-office hits. When Elvis was drafted there had been talk of him possibly joining the Special Services, where he could have sung and retained some rapport with the public. But Colonel Parker, his manager, and RCA were convinced that he should serve his country as a regular soldier, claiming that the public would respect Elvis as a man if he went in as a buck private. Now Elvis was afraid he might have lost the support of his fans.

While we were parked, one of the *Fräuleins* who lived in the pension passed the car. She greeted me and then, when she glanced at Elvis, her mouth dropped open in disbelief.

3

Time had become my enemy. Elvis was due to return to the States on March 1, 1960. I had only a few months left to spend as much time with him as I could.

Every minute I wasn't with him, I thought of him. My life was now dominated by him and yet there were times when I would be disappointed by him. One evening he told me he would call and didn't. When I finally heard from him the next day, he said, "Hi, Baby. Do you think you can come over tonight?"

"What happened last night? You were supposed to call."

"I was? Oh shit." He had been concentrating on his karate lesson and had forgotten.

I had to learn not to take his words to heart. It was disappointing, but it was just his way.

Elvis's calls usually came after seven to let me know that I'd be picked up around eight. I had to dress quickly, trying to find some way to appear older than my age. His father was concerned about Elvis being with a minor. My clothes were all young and unsophisticated skirts and sweaters. At times I'd borrow my mother's clothes and hope everyone would assume that I was at least sixteen.

As I got to know Elvis, I learned that when he wasn't at the base, he virtually lived as a recluse. He had little choice. The moment he stepped out of the door there was a giant mob scene around him. Even going to see a local movie required elaborate planning. Someone would drive Elvis's car in front of the house. He would then run out, hurdle the fence, and duck into the car before any of his fans could start begging him for autographs. There were always crowds after him, calling, standing outside the house, literally charging at him when he entered any public place.

Many evenings when Elvis had early morning calls it was either Lamar Fike, a friend whom Elvis had brought over from the States, or Vernon Presley who chauffeured me to and from 14 Goethestrasse.

One particular evening when neither Lamar nor Vernon was able to drive me home, Elvis had a "friend" whom we'll call Kurt (not his real name) take me.

Kurt was driving me from Elvis's home back to Wiesbaden. I was tired and dozing off. All of a sudden, I felt the road get bumpy. I opened my eyes.

"What's wrong?" I asked.

"You'll find out," he said, turning his head away.

We had driven off the highway onto a dirt road. I could see the lights of one distant house, and the rest was all blackness. I began to get frightened. "What's going on?" I inquired, confused. By then Kurt had stopped the car and shut off the ignition.

I repeated my question, but Kurt didn't answer. Instead, he turned and grabbed me, trying to kiss me. I pushed him away, struggling. He threw me down on the seat.

Panicked, I begged, "Don't! Leave me alone!" I started fighting. I kicked one door open and opened the driver's door with my hand while simultaneously banging the horn, hitting the lights, and scratching at his face. Out of frustration and fear of being caught, he finally gave up.

The rest of the way home, he never said a word. I just sat there sobbing, disbelieving, praying that I would get home safely.

Three days passed from that night before I heard from Elvis. My parents knew something was wrong; however, I couldn't tell them Kurt tried to attack me because I would never be allowed to ride with him again. If I didn't, how would I get to and from Elvis's if Lamar and Vernon weren't available? My imagination ran wild. I was afraid to tell Elvis because I thought Kurt was his friend. I began to think that perhaps Elvis knew what Kurt had attempted. Maybe I was just a plaything to Elvis, someone to pass around to Kurt, or anyone else who wanted me. I was tortured by my thoughts.

Finally, Kurt called and said Elvis wanted to see me. I had no choice but to go with him.

During the drive to Bad Nauheim, Kurt made no

mention of what had transpired between us, and neither did I. I said nothing. I was very apprehensive being with him. I didn't know, when he removed his hand from the steering wheel, if he was going to try to touch me, or just what was on his mind. I had no choice but to tell Elvis.

That evening, when we were alone in his room, Elvis asked me if anything was wrong.

My voice was trembling. I could hardly get the words out.

When I finally did tell him, Elvis went berserk. "I'm going to kill him," he shouted. He paced the floor, cursing Kurt. I was his little girl, Elvis said, and he had never gone all the way with me. Now this other guy, this so-called friend of his, had tried to rape me. I listened as he shouted, secretly relieved at his response. How could I ever have doubted Elvis?

Elvis was so incensed, it took me the whole evening to calm him down. I finally convinced him that we had to keep Kurt's attack secret from my parents, or I'd never be allowed to come back. Elvis held me tightly, as if trying to take the painful memory away. He felt guilty for having put me in such a dangerous position.

From that time on, Kurt was virtually excluded from Elvis's life. I don't think Elvis ever told him why, but Kurt must have known. He rarely came around after that.

I began to realize that Elvis expected total loyalty from his friends. If he was betrayed, he would just cut that person out of his life.

Vernon was now sporting a neatly trimmed mustache that, according to Elvis, Dee Stanley had encouraged him to grow. Our conversations in the car were somewhat perfunctory, and I always sensed he'd just as soon be doing something else, like spending the time with Dee, who sometimes accompanied him.

These days when I arrived at 14 Goethestrasse I'd often find Elvis upstairs studying the ancient art of karate with his instructor or downstairs in the living room proudly demonstrating new moves to his entourage, who stood about marveling at his mastery of this newly popularized art form.

Elvis also spent hours with a half-mad German masseur who had him convinced he could rejuvenate facial skin with his secret treatments, Elvis having always been self-conscious about some large pores on his face. Joe Esposito ribbed Elvis, saying, "What the hell's he doing that's so special? You look the same to me." Defensively, Elvis shot back, "Well damn! He says it'll take some time before you see the results." Vernon interjected: "Time? Yeah, probably enough time to bankrupt us all by what he's charging. I wouldn't trust him farther than I could throw him."

Always a center of activity at the house was Elvis's grandmother, whom he nicknamed Dodger. Elvis had come up with the name when he was a small boy of five and, during a temper tantrum, had thrown a baseball, missing her head by inches. Elvis jokingly said, "She dodged out of the way so fast." He started calling her Dodger from that moment.

Grandma took care of the household, did the cooking, kept everyone and everything under control. She had the air of a person with a firm purpose in life, which, in

Elvis's case, was to make sure he was very well cared for. When I sought quiet while Elvis practiced karate, Dodger's room was a place to escape to. We'd sit for hours and she would tell me about the old days, about Gladys and her boundless love for Elvis, about the grim struggle the Presleys had waged for survival. She had been with Vernon and Gladys from the time of Elvis's birth, helping out when Gladys took jobs to contribute to the family's support. A strong woman, Grandma had prevailed when her husband had walked out on her, leaving her with five children. She wanted you to believe she held a grudge against J. D. Presley, but Dodger's was a forgiving heart and I believe she still cared for him.

She helped raise Elvis as if he were her own son, somewhat spoiling him as grandmothers do. She always rushed to his defense when she felt Gladys was too stern. Dodger said to me, "Gladys always called me Mrs. Presley from the time I first met her until she breathed her last breath. One day Elvis came running in and said, 'Hi, Minnie!' I felt so sorry for that young'un. Gladys rose up, took her hand to that boy, and said, 'Don't you ever call her by her first name. That's disrespectful. She's your grandma.' He cried for an hour. I went in and said, 'Son, it'll be all right. She was just doing what she thought was right. Now you go in and apologize to her.' Poor little boy looked at me with those blue eyes. So pitiful. Oh, she could be hard on im. He was a good boy, though. Never really got into any trouble, always came right home from school and did his chores. Yes, and Gladys would watch over him like a hawk, so scared he'd be hurt. He wanted so bad to play football at school."

Grandma rocked back and forth in her chair, seeing something in the past that made her start picking at the bobby pins in her hair. She reached for her little box of snuff, took a dip, situated it just right, and then continued to reminisce. "Yes, he loved sports."

"Then why didn't he go out for any, Grandma?"

"Oh no. Gladys wouldn't have that. She'd tell me, 'Oh, Mrs. Presley, I couldn't stand it if Elvis got hurt. It would kill me. I've watched how they play out there in those fields. They get real rough. I think they enjoy hurtin' each other. Elvis isn't like that. He'd get out there and he'd be like a wounded bird in a pack of wild dogs. Not my young'un.' " Gladys's constant effort to protect Elvis, I learned, was the result of her anguish over the death of Elvis's twin brother Jesse Garon.

I came to love Dodger and what she represented— compassion and total devotion to her family.

My biggest problem in those days was that Elvis and I never seemed to have enough time alone. People were always dropping by, standing around the living room talking and laughing, until Elvis came down from his room. As soon as he appeared, the room would become silent until he revealed his mood. No one, including myself, dared joke around unless he laughed and then we all laughed.

Because I had to share the little time I had with Elvis with so many others, I began to feel jealous and possessive. It was only late in the evening, when we were in his bedroom, that I was truly happy.

We had a nightly ritual. At about ten or eleven, Elvis would glance at me and look toward the stairs. Then, naively assuming that nobody knew where I was headed, I'd casually proceed to his bedroom, where I'd lie on his bed, impatiently waiting for him to appear. When he joined me, he'd lie as close to me as he could. "I love you," I whispered. "Shhh," he said as he put his fingers to my lips. "I don't really understand what it is I'm feeling. I've grown to love you, Cilla. Daddy keeps reminding me of your age and that it can't be possible . . . When I go home . . . Only time will tell."

Each night that I was with him he entrusted a little more of himself—his doubts, his secrets, and his frustrations. It was a lot to expect an impressionable fourteen-year-old to understand, but I tried. I felt his pain over his mother's death. I ached over his desire to become a great actor like his idols Marlon Brando, James Dean, Karl Malden, and Rod Steiger. I was concerned about his fears that he might not regain the popularity he felt he'd lost by serving in the Army. And I reveled in his laughter when he asked, "What if one day I end up back driving a Crown Electric truck? Wouldn't that be something?"

I was there for him, to listen, to hold his hand, or to make a funny face that would turn his frown into a smile.

Sometimes Elvis would enter his bedroom in high spirits. I longed for those nights when he'd shut off the lights and lie close beside me.

"Sweetness," he would say, putting his arms around me. "You're so pretty, Honey." And then we'd kiss long, deep, passionate kisses, and his caresses would leave me weak with desire.

Nights when his mood was calm and peaceful, he would describe his ideal woman and tell me how perfectly I fit this image.

He liked soft-spoken brunettes with blue eyes. He wanted to mold me to his opinions and preferences. Despite his reputation for being a rebel, he held the traditional view of relationships. A woman had her place, and it was the man who took the initiative.

Fidelity was very important to him, especially on the woman's part. He constantly reminded me that his girl had to be completely constant. He admitted that he was concerned about Anita. She was a Memphis beauty queen and television personality. Elvis said that lately her letters had become very impersonal, and he suspected she had been with another man.

Despite his moralizing, I feared Elvis wasn't always faithful to me. His bantering with some of the other girls at his house made me think that he might be intimately familiar with them.

One evening he was playing the piano for the regular group, plus a couple of English girls. When he picked up his guitar, he looked around, but couldn't seem to find his pick.

"Anybody seen my guitar pick?" he asked.

One of the English girls looked up and smiled. "It's upstairs on the night table next to your bed. I'll get it."

All eyes, including mine, zeroed in on her as she made

her way up the stairs, aware that she was now the center of attention.

Furious at his obvious betrayal, I turned to him, but he was avoiding my gaze by looking down at his guitar, plucking it as if it needed tuning. Then he burst into "Lawdy, Miss Clawdy."

Without a pick, his fingers must have hurt badly, but no matter what, he wasn't about to put that guitar down. He knew he was in trouble.

After he'd finished a medley of songs, Elvis excused himself and retreated into the kitchen, with me right behind him.

"Have you been with her?" I demanded.

"No," Elvis insisted.

"Then how did she know where your guitar pick and room were?"

"She was over one night, and I mentioned how dirty the place was," he answered, a boyish grin on his face. "She offered to clean it, simple as that."

Despite his declaration of innocence, I was not reassured. He was the sexual idol of millions and could choose whomever he wanted, whenever he wanted. I quickly learned, for my own survival, not to ask too many questions.

4

As the weeks passed, school became an unbearable chore. After getting to bed so late, I found it difficult to rise at seven and almost impossible to concentrate. But I knew that if I ever complained about being too tired, or was late for school, my parents would use the fact to put a stop to my seeing Elvis.

My study habits became worse. I was failing algebra and German, and barely passing history and English. At the end of the fall semester, I altered the D-minus grade on my report card to a B-plus, praying my father would never consult the teacher. I kept telling myself that I would do better, that I'd catch up, but my concentration was totally on Elvis.

One night when I went to see him, I fell asleep while waiting for him to finish his karate class. When he came downstairs and saw how exhausted I was, he asked, "Priscilla, how many hours of sleep are you getting?"

After a second, I said, "About four or five hours a night. But I'll be fine," I added quickly. "I'm just a little extra tired tonight because we had some tests at school today."

Elvis looked thoughtful, and then said, "Come upstairs a minute. I have something for you." He led me up to his room, where he placed a handful of small white pills in the palm of my hand. "I want you to take these; they'll help you stay awake during the day. Just take one when you feel a little drowsy, no more than one, though, or you'll be doing handstands down the hallway."

"What are they?" I asked.

"You don't need to know what they are; they give them to us when we go on maneuvers. If I didn't have them, I'd never make it through the day myself. But it's okay, they're safe," he told me. "Put them away and don't tell anyone you have them, and don't take them every day. Just when you need a little more energy."

Elvis honestly thought he was doing me a favor by giving me the pills, and I'm sure the thought never entered his mind that they could be harmful to him or me.

I didn't take the pills. I put them in a small box with various items I had started to collect, such as cigar holders and little personal notes he had given me, and hid the box in a drawer.

Later I learned that the pills were Dexedrine, which Elvis had first discovered in the Army. A sergeant had given several men pills to help them stay awake while on guard duty. Elvis, who was accustomed to living the life of an entertainer and who despised rising at dawn, began taking the pills to get him through the long dreary hours of Army life. He told me he'd begun taking sleeping pills shortly before he'd been drafted. He dreaded insomnia and feared sleepwalking, which had plagued him periodically since childhood.

In fact, as a boy, he'd once sleepwalked straight out of his apartment, dressed only in his underwear. A neighbor woke him, and, embarrassed, he ran back into the house. Another time, he nearly fell out of a window. Consequently, to avoid accidents, he slept with his parents until he was grown, and he feared his sleepwalking habit for the rest of his life. It was one of the reasons he usually had someone sleeping with him.

Years later, I learned that someone had been employed in Germany to watch over him throughout the night.

It was already Christmas 1959, and I had no idea what to get Elvis. I walked through the crowded streets of Wiesbaden, window-shopping, trying to get ideas. Picking out gifts for the family had always been easy, since we always knew exactly what was wanted or needed; in fact, we often made our gifts for one another. On this occasion my father gave me thirty-five dollars to spend on Elvis, and it seemed a vast amount to me when I set out on this freezing cold day. I was disabused of the notion when I priced a beautiful hand-made cigar box with porcelain outlining a decorative design. Elvis, a cigar smoker, would have loved it. But after the shopkeeper told me the price—650 Deutsche marks or $155—all I walked out with was my expensive taste.

It was snowing heavily and I hurried into another shop, this one full of bright toys, including a solidly built toy German train that I could imagine Elvis instantly setting up in his living room. But the train cost 2,000 Deutsche marks.

Heading home in the dark, on the verge of tears, I spotted a music store, where a pair of bongo drums inlaid with gleaming brass were displayed in the window. They were forty dollars, but the clerk took mercy on me and sold them for thirty-five. As I headed home I was beset by a thousand doubts, convinced that the drums were the least romantic of gifts.

I must have asked Joe Esposito and Lamar Fike twenty times if they thought the drums were appropriate. "Oh sure," Joe said. "Anything you give him, he'll like." I still wasn't convinced.

On the night we exchanged gifts, Elvis emerged from his dad's room and drew me to one corner of the living room, where he handed me a small wrapped box, in it, a delicate gold watch with a diamond set on the lid and a ring with a pearl bracketed by two diamonds.

I had never owned anything so beautiful, nor had any smile ever warmed me as Elvis's did then. "I'll cherish these forever," I told him, and he made me put them on right away and took me around to show everyone.

I waited as long as possible to give Elvis my present. Laughing, he said, "Bongos! Just what I always wanted!" Elvis could see that I didn't believe him; he was better at giving than receiving. "Charlie," he persisted, "didn't I need some bongos?"

Motioning for me to sit next to him at the piano, he started playing "I'll Be Home for Christmas" with such emotion that I couldn't look up for fear he'd see I was crying. When at last I couldn't resist meeting his eyes, I saw that he too was holding back tears.

It was not until many days later that I discovered a whole closetful of bongo drums—mine not included—in the basement. That my white elephants had not been consigned to dark oblivion but stood prominently displayed beside his guitar made me love him all the more.

As the days passed I began to dread the day of Elvis's departure. By January he was already packing, and each night I spent with him became more precious than the one before.

Then, just as the weather turned freezing cold, Elvis was sent out on field maneuvers for ten days, and if there was anything Elvis hated, it was having to sleep outside on the frozen ground.

The morning after he left, it began to snow and by afternoon it was a blizzard. As Michelle and I were driving home from school with my mother, I turned on the radio, just in time to hear a late-breaking news bulletin.

"Sorry to interrupt, folks, but it was just reported that Corporal Elvis Presley has been rushed from field maneuvers to a hospital in Frankfurt, suffering from an acute attack of tonsillitis. Elvis, if you're listening, we all hope you get well real soon."

Frantic with worry, I called the hospital, hoping to learn more about his condition. To my surprise, when the operator heard my name she put me right through, saying Corporal Presley had left word to do so if I called.

"I'm a sick man, Little One," Elvis rasped. "I need you by my side. If it's okay with your folks, I'll send Lamar for you right now."

Of course my parents gave me permission to go to the hospital, and an hour later I entered his room, just as the nurse was leaving. Elvis was propped up in bed with a thermometer in his mouth, surrounded by dozens of floral arrangements.

The moment the nurse was gone, Elvis took the thermometer out of his mouth, lit a match, and carefully held it under the thermometer. Then he stuck the thermometer back in his mouth and slumped down on the bed just as the door opened and the nurse returned, carrying in even more flowers.

Smiling warmly to her famous patient, she took the thermometer out of Elvis's mouth, looked at it, and gasped, "A hundred and three. Why, Elvis, you're really sick. I'm afraid you'll have to stay here at least a week."

Elvis nodded mutely as the nurse fluffed up his pillows, filled his water glass, and left the room. Then he burst out laughing, jumped out of bed, and took me in his arms.

He despised maneuvers, and since the weather was so bad and everyone was so worried about his voice, his answer was tonsillitis. Already susceptible to catching colds, Elvis learned to dramatize his sickness with a little flick of a match.

5

IT WAS March 1, 1960, the night before Elvis was to leave Germany to return to the States.

We were lying on his bed, our arms around each other. I was in a state of complete despair.

"Oh, Elvis," I said, "I just wish there were some way you could take me with you. I can't stand the thought of life without you. I love you so much."

I began sobbing, my anguish overcoming my control.

"Shhh, Baby," Elvis whispered. "Try to calm down. There's nothing we can do."

"I'm just afraid you'll forget me the moment you land," I cried.

He smiled and kissed me gently. "I'm not going to forget you, Cilla. I've never felt this way about another girl. I love you."

"You do?" I was stunned. Elvis had said that I was

special before, but he'd never said that he loved me. I wanted so badly to believe him, but I was frightened of getting hurt. I'd read some of Anita's letters, and I was sure Elvis was on his way back to her open arms.

Holding me close, he said, "I'm torn with the feelings I have for you. I don't know what to do. Maybe being away will help me understand what I really feel."

That night our lovemaking took on a new urgency. Would I ever see him again, be in his arms the way I had been nearly every night for the past six months? I missed him already. I could not bear the thought of the night ending and our saying goodbye for what I thought would be the last time. I wept and wept until my body ached with pain.

For the last time I begged him to consummate our love. It would have been so easy for him. I was young, vulnerable, desperately in love, and he could have taken complete advantage of me. But he quietly said, "No. Someday we will, Priscilla, but not now. You're just too young."

I lay awake all that night and early the next morning I was back at 14 Goethestrasse, lost in the midst of a large group of people milling about the living room. They were waiting to say goodbye to Elvis, who was upstairs finishing his last-minute packing. Knowing that I alone would be accompanying him to the airport gave me little comfort.

When Elvis came downstairs, he laughed and joked with everyone there. Finally, after saying his last good-bye, Elvis turned to me. "Okay, Little One, it's time to go."

I nodded glumly and followed him out the door. Oblivious to the drizzling rain, hundreds of fans were waiting outside. When they saw Elvis they went crazy, begging him to sign autographs. When he finished he jumped into the waiting car and pulled me in behind him. As the door slammed, the driver accelerated and we sped toward the airport.

We rode for a long while in silence, both of us lost in thought. Elvis was gazing out the window, frowning over the falling rain. "I know it's not going to be easy for you to go back to being a schoolgirl again after being with me, Cilla, but you've got to. I don't want you to be sitting around moping after I leave, Little One."

I started to protest, but he silenced me. "Try to have a good time, write to me every chance you get. I'll look forward to your letters. Get pink stationery. Address them to Joe. That way I'll know they're from you. I want you to promise me you'll stay the way you are. Untouched, as I left you."

"I will," I promised.

"I'll look for you from the top of the ramp. I don't want to see a sad face. Give me a little smile. I'll take that with me."

Then, handing me his combat jacket and the sergeant's stripes he'd recently been awarded, he said, "I want you to have these. It shows you belong to me." After that, he held me tight.

As we approached the airport, the cheers of the waiting crowds grew louder. We drove as close to the runway as possible, then Elvis turned to me and said, "This is it, Baby."

We got out as cameras flashed, reporters shouted, and screaming fans pressed toward us. Elvis held my hand and walked across the runway apron until the guard, who was there to escort Elvis to the plane, stopped me from going further.

Elvis gave me a brief hug and whispered, "Don't worry, I'll call you when I get home, Baby, promise."

I nodded, but before I could answer, we were pulled apart as the crowd rushed in. I was swept away by hundreds of fans, pushing and pulling, trying to get to him. I cried, "Elvis!" but he never heard me.

He ran up the boarding steps. Then he turned and waved to the crowd, his eyes searching for me. I waved frantically, as did hundreds of other fans, yet he found me, and for one more brief moment, our eyes locked. Then he disappeared. Just like that.

My parents came to the airport to drive me back to Wiesbaden. During the long ride I was silent.

6

FOR THE NEXT two days I locked myself in my room, unable to eat, unable to sleep. Finally my mother said, "This isn't going to help. Moping around here isn't going to bring him back. He's gone. He'll be getting into his new life, and so should you."

I forced myself to go to school and found myself swamped by photographers and reporters who were calling me "the girl he left behind" and barraging me with questions.

"How old are you, Miss Beaulieu?"

"I'm, uh—"

"Your records show you're only in the ninth grade."

"Well, ah, yes, that—"

"How long have you known Mr. Presley?"

"About . . . just a few months."

"What is your relationship with him?"

"We're . . . just friends."

"Has he called you since he returned?"

"No, but—"

"Did you know he's seeing Nancy Sinatra?"

"What?"

"Nancy Sinatra."

Suddenly feeling sick, I excused myself and left.

Each day there were calls from the United States, with offers of first-class round-trip tickets for me to appear on TV. I declined these as well as offers from top European magazines requesting interviews and photo sessions. Letters poured in from lonesome GIs all over the world. I had attracted their attention, perhaps as a soldier's sweetheart. I also received letters from Elvis's fans, some friendly and some disheartened that maybe they had lost him.

Days passed into weeks and I became more and more resigned to the fact that Elvis was now dating Nancy Sinatra and had completely forgotten me. Twenty-one days after he left, the phone rang at three o'clock in the morning. I jumped out of bed, ran to answer it, and heard his wonderful voice.

"Hi, Baby. How's my Little Girl?"

"Oh, Elvis, I'm fine," I said. "Only I miss you so. I thought you had forgotten me. Everyone was saying you would."

"I told you I'd call, Cilla," he assured me.

"I know, Elvis, but there were photographers here and reporters and they kept asking me questions, and—oh, Elvis, is it true you're seeing Nancy Sinatra?"

"Hold it. Hold it! Slow down," he said, laughing. "No it's not true that I'm seeing Nancy Sinatra."

"But they said you were."

"Don't believe everything you hear, Little Girl. You'll find people trying to stir up trouble, just to make you upset. She's a friend, Baby, just a friend. I'm appearing on her father's show, and it was all set up for her to be here at my press conference when I returned to the States. I miss you, Baby. I think about you all the time."

After that first phone call, I spent all my time writing and rewriting letters to him, but he never wrote back. Then one day he called, sounding very excited.

"I'm leaving for California in two days, Baby. I'm starting my first movie since the Army."

All I could think about was whether he'd fall in love with his costar. As casually as I could, I asked, "Who's your leading lady?"

Elvis burst out laughing. "You don't have to worry, Baby, I haven't met her yet, but I hear she's real tall. Her name's Juliet Prowse. She's a dancer and she's engaged to Frank Sinatra."

Relieved, I asked, "What's the name of the film?"

"Wouldn't you know it," he answered, "*G.I. Blues*. I *think* it'll be pretty good. I'm a little concerned that there are too many songs in it, but I think it'll work out. It had better, or I'll have a few choice words to say."

A few weeks later Elvis called again. His enthusiasm for *G.I. Blues* had turned to bitter disappointment.

"I just finished looping the goddamn picture," he said dejectedly. "And I hate it. They have about twelve songs in it that aren't worth a cat's ass," he said angrily, and then added, "I just had a meeting with Colonel Parker about it. I want half of them out. I feel like a goddamn idiot breaking into a song while I'm talking to some chick on a train."

"Well, what'd the Colonel say?" I asked.

"Hell, what could he say? I'm locked into this thing. Already been paid," he complained. "They seemed to think it's wonderful. I'm goddamn miserable."

"Maybe the next one will be better," I said.

"Yeah, yeah," he said, starting to calm down. "The Colonel's requested better scripts. It's just this is my first film since I've been back and it's a joke." There was a long pause as static filled the line. Finally Elvis said, "I gotta go, Cilla, and I can barely hear you. I'll call you soon, be good, I love you."

I was living in a state of suspended animation, waiting for Elvis's infrequent calls. There was never a pattern to them. He would phone out of the blue after three weeks—or three months. He always did most of the talking, chatting about his current film or his costar. Occasionally, he'd talk about Anita, saying their relationship wasn't what he had expected when he returned from the Army. He was no longer sure he wanted to be with her. I didn't know where I stood. Time and distance had created doubts and questions; I wanted to ask him, "Where do I fit in your life? Or do I?"

Elvis was still mentioning that he really wanted me to see Graceland, especially at Christmas, when it was its most beautiful. He said I'd meet Alberta, the maid. Elvis called her Alberta VO5. He laughed and said, "I'll tell her, 'O Five, I've got a little girl I want you to meet.'"

This gave me some hope of a future. I wanted to believe him when he said he still cared for me. But during the periods when I did not hear from him, I couldn't help but doubt that I would ever see him again. I heard his latest hit record, "(Marie's the Name) His Latest Flame," and felt sure that he'd fallen in love with a girl named Marie.

That summer, Paul Anka was on a European tour. He was to make a guest appearance at a nearby Air Force facility in Wiesbaden. I slyly arranged for my mother to drop me off at the time specified for his arrival. My intentions, unknown to her, were highly contrived and they had to do, strictly, with Elvis. I wanted to ask him if by chance he knew Elvis and if Elvis had ever mentioned me. But when he got out of his car he was surrounded by fans, and I was too shy to push through the crowd to speak to him.

I gleaned every bit of news about Elvis that I could. I listened constantly to the overseas radio and scanned every article in *The Stars and Stripes* newspaper. But each story about Elvis I read only upset me all the more. Besides Anita, he seemed to be romantically linked with many beautiful young starlets in Hollywood—Tuesday Weld, Juliet Prowse, and Anne Helm, among others.

I wrote him: "I need you and want you in every way and, believe me, there's no one else . . . I wish to God I were with you now. I need you and all your love more than anything in this world."

7

It was a cold, snowy day in March 1962, nearly two years since Elvis had left Germany. In the late afternoon, I received a call from him. It had been months since we last spoke.

"I'd like to make arrangements for you to visit me in Los Angeles," he said. "Do you think we can work it out?"

Stunned, I blurted, "What? I'm not sure. Oh God, I wasn't expecting this. It's going to take some time, some planning."

I didn't think my father could ever be persuaded to let me go. There were several phone calls with Elvis trying to say all the right words to please my parents. I had separate talks with my mother, hoping she'd help me convince Dad.

Once again Elvis met every one of Dad's demands: that we wait until I was out of school for the summer, that Elvis send me a first-class round-trip ticket, that he send my parents an exact itinerary of my daily activities for the two weeks I'd be in Los Angeles, that I be constantly chaperoned, and that I write my parents every day.

The next few months might as well have been years. I marked off each day on the calendar until we would be together.

When the plane landed in Los Angeles, I found the terminal bustling with vacationing students. But I easily spotted Joe Esposito, who was still working for Elvis.

It was good to see Joe. His big smile and warm embrace were comforting. I loved hearing him tell me I looked great. I didn't think I did. The last time Elvis saw me, I had been fourteen years old and five pounds lighter. I was afraid that he might be disappointed when he saw me, that he might send me home the next day.

I got my first glimpse of Los Angeles when we drove in from the airport. It was beautiful, a far cry from the drabness of postwar Germany. As we passed the MGM studios in Culver City, Joe said, "That's where Elvis films most of his movies." Soon we were speeding along the legendary Sunset Strip and through the large wrought-iron gates of Bel Air. I was entering a world I'd never experienced. Every home along the winding road seemed grander than the one before.

We turned in at Elvis's house on Bellagio Road, a large home modeled after an Italian villa. We were greeted by Elvis's butler, who introduced himself as Jimmy and said, "Mr. P is in the den." As we walked through the door, I could hear loud music playing and people laughing. Joe led me downstairs.

Before entering, I took a deep breath. The years of waiting were now over.

In the dim light I saw people lounging on a couch and others standing over a jukebox, selecting songs. Then I spotted Elvis, dressed in dark trousers, a white shirt, and a black captain's hat. He was leaning over a pool table, ready to make a shot. I wanted to run to him, but this roomful of people was not the setting I had dreamed of for our first meeting. I continued to stand there, watching him.

He looked up and saw me and after a slight pause his face lit with a smile. "There she is!" he shouted, throwing down his cue stick. "There's Priscilla!"

He made his way over to me, picked me up in his arms, and kissed me. I held onto him for as long as I could—until he put me down. "It's about time," he said, joking. "Where have you been all my life?"

Aware that every eye in the room was on us, I was uncomfortable and embarrassed. I quickly wiped the tears from my face before anyone noticed. Elvis took my hand and introduced me around, and then we sat down together.

"Baby, I'm so glad you're here," he kept saying. "I can't wait to show you around. You've grown up. You look great. Let me look at you. Stand up."

As his eyes surveyed me, I became increasingly self-conscious, and I didn't want him looking too long. He might find flaws.

He looked terrific, although I was surprised to see that the blondish hair he'd had in the Army was now dyed black. He looked thinner, happier.

"Don't go away," he said. He kissed me lovingly, then returned to the pool table to finish his game. The night seemed to go slowly—too slowly. While Elvis continued his game a few of the girls eased their way over to me and started talking. They said Elvis threw parties almost every night.

Hearing this and watching him as the night progressed, I felt out of touch with his new life, even though the girls told me he talked about me often and even showed my pictures around.

Playing pool, Elvis laughed and joked around, and when one of the girls bent over the table to attempt a shot, Elvis poked her in the backside with his pool cue. She shrieked in surprise and everyone laughed—everyone except me. I couldn't help noticing that there had been a slight change in Elvis. He'd left Germany a gentle, sensitive, and insecure boy; through the course of the evening I'd see that he now was mischievous and self-confident to the point of cockiness.

He also seemed quick to anger. When a girl cautioned him to watch out for a glass that was perched precariously on the edge of the pool table, he shot her a dirty look, as if to tell her, "Move the glass yourself."

I felt a surge of uneasiness. I was unsure of what to do or say. Between shots he'd come over and give me an affectionate kiss, ask if I was all right, and then move back for his next shot. Meanwhile, the curious stares of his female admirers never left me.

It was after 12:30 A.M. when Elvis finally sat down next to me. Now it was like the old days in Germany: He was suggesting that we go to his bedroom. "Up the stairs, the first door to your right," he said. "The lights are on. I'll be right up." I started to rise. "Wait a few minutes, until I get up and leave," he said. "That way it won't look so obvious."

I wasn't sure if I liked that. I knew he was protecting me, but there were so many pretty girls around, I wanted to make sure everyone knew he was mine—at least for as long as I was here. I'd waited too long to be discreet. I got up, stretched a little, and politely said good night to everyone, hoping they would know *exactly* where I was going.

I ran up the stairs and easily found Elvis's bedroom. How different it was from his ordinary-looking quarters in Germany. I never imagined him living in such luxury—thick carpets, exquisite furnishings—but the room had a welcoming, lived-in feeling.

And then my eyes fell on the king-size bed in the middle of the room. I immediately thought of how many women might have slept there . . . whose bodies he had embraced and fondled . . . and even worse, whose lips had passionately pressed his and driven him to ecstasy. I couldn't think about it anymore.

I walked over to the French doors, which overlooked the driveway, and saw Elvis's guests exchanging good nights as they got into their cars. Knowing he'd probably be coming up soon, I rushed into the large adjoining bathroom.

Within ten minutes, I had jumped in and out of the bathtub, combed my hair, brushed my teeth, and dusted my entire body with some powder I'd found in the medicine cabinet. I put on my favorite blue pajamas and stood motionless before the door leading to the bedroom. I was so apprehensive that I was unable to open the door. This was the moment I had both longed for and feared. I sat down on a chair and remembered that when I'd been fourteen, Elvis had said that I was "too young." Now that I was sixteen I tried to imagine just what this new Elvis, whom I hardly knew at all, might be expecting of me.

About fifteen minutes later, I heard him as he opened the bedroom door, yelling down to his cousin, Billy Smith, who also worked for him: "Don't let me sleep later than three tomorrow, Billy." Then I heard him close the door, lock it, and call out, "Where are you, Baby?"

"I'm in the bathroom," I shouted. "I'll be just a few more minutes."

"Don't take too long. I want to see my girl."

I still couldn't move.

He called again: "What are you doing in there, Cilla? No one takes this long to get ready for bed."

It was the moment of truth: Taking a deep breath, I opened the door and walked out. Elvis was lying on the bed, facing me. I walked slowly toward him, climbed into the bed, and lay down next to him. Our faces were only inches apart. It was such an unexpected moment of tenderness that I was mesmerized looking into his eyes. We lay there for what seemed like a long time, staring at each other until our eyes filled with tears.

Elvis softly touched my face. "God," he whispered. "You don't know how much I've missed you. You've been an inspiration to me. Don't ask me why, but I haven't been able to put you out of my mind since I left you in Germany. It's been the one thing that's kept me going."

I couldn't hold back any longer: Tears streamed down my face. Elvis took me in his arms and held me close, but I couldn't get close enough. If I could have gotten *inside* him, I would have.

"It's gonna be all right, Baby. I promise you. You're here now and that's all that matters. We'll have a good time and not think about you going back."

As we lay in the dim light, he soon discovered that I was still as untouched as he'd left me two years before. Relieved and pleased, he told me how much this meant to him. It was as if every feeling I had as a woman began to emerge, and I began kissing him passionately. I wanted him—I was ready to submit entirely to him. He returned my passion. Then, abruptly, he stopped.

"Wait a minute, Baby," he said, speaking softly. "This can get out of hand."

"Is there anything wrong?" I was fearful that I wasn't

pleasing him. He shook his head, kissed me again, then gently put my hand on him. I could feel for myself just how much he desired me, emotionally and physically. He pressed his body to mine and it felt wonderful.

"Elvis, I want you."

He put his finger to my lips and whispered, "Not yet, not now. We have a lot to look forward to. I'm not going to spoil you. I just want to keep you the way you are for now. There'll be a right time and place, and when the moment comes, I'll know it."

Although confused, I wasn't about to argue. He made it clear that this was what he wanted. He made it sound so romantic, and, in a strange way, it *was* something to look forward to—just as he had said.

Later that night he told me that I had to stay with friends of his, George and Shirley Barris. Although I protested, Elvis said, "I don't want to go back on my promise to your father. Besides, if he found out you were staying with me, he'd make you go right home." It didn't make any sense, but I got out of bed and Elvis had Joe drive me over to the Barrises' house, where I would spend the night. Reluctantly.

Later I found out through one of the wives whom I had befriended the reason for my spending that first night with George and Shirley. Apparently Anita had been sent back to Memphis the day before, and Elvis was taking precautions to avoid any awkward situations for himself that might have resulted from late-night phone calls.

8

It was after three o'clock the next afternoon when Elvis called. "Alan's on his way to pick you up," he said. Alan Fortas was another of his employees.

When we arrived at Elvis's house, I found him upstairs dressing. As soon as he saw me, he kissed me and asked, "How would you like to go to Las Vegas? We could really have fun and I could show you around my favorite places." Not understanding his contradiction regarding my staying with the Barrises the night before, and feeling uneasy asking any questions, I answered, "I'd love to. When?"

"Tonight. We'll load up the bus and head out about midnight, arrive in the morning, sleep all day, and see the shows and party all night."

Excitement was in the air—*Las Vegas*. I'd never

dreamed of going there and I really didn't know what to expect. Actually, I really didn't care where we went as long as I was with him.

I had two immediate concerns. One, I didn't know if I could afford—or at my age should even wear—the glamorous clothes suitable for Vegas, but Elvis said not to worry, Alan would take me shopping that afternoon.

It was a strange experience, shopping with someone I barely knew, particularly a man. He seemed as uncomfortable as I but assured me we would find something. He was familiar with all of the boutiques and took me to Saks Fifth Avenue as well.

As I selected a couple of outfits I worried about my other concern: the promised daily letter to my parents. How would I explain Las Vegas postmarks? I couldn't. But I could prewrite letters for the time we were gone, number them one through seven, and have Jimmy mail them from Los Angeles daily. My problems were solved. On to Las Vegas!

That evening Elvis's front lawn was alive with activity. There seemed to be people everywhere. The huge bus that George Barris had custom-designed for Elvis stood in the driveway. The guys streamed in and out of it, loading suitcases, records, a stereo system, and cases of Pepsi-Cola. All the preparations and excitement made it look as if Elvis were moving out, but in fact he always traveled this way. He was still uneasy about flying—a fear he later conquered—and felt much more relaxed driving. Because we didn't know how long we'd stay, Alan and Gene Smith brought along whatever Elvis enjoyed, so he would feel as comfortable as if he were at home. I was happy. It was the first time we'd be together without restrictions or curfews.

Just before midnight, they all gathered around the big bus; it was time to say goodbye to any visitors the regulars were leaving behind.

Elvis was dressed in a white shirt, black pants, black racing gloves, and his ever-present yachting cap. As we pulled away, he yelled out the window, "We shall return," and we hit the highway for Las Vegas, Nevada. I didn't know what I was headed for, but I loved the idea of adventure.

And I felt proud; there was Gene to my right, me in the center, and Elvis driving. I learned that Elvis always preferred driving at night; it was cooler and there was less traffic. He came alive at night. There was a big difference between the daytime Elvis and the nocturnal Elvis. When the sun went down another personality took over, and on this particular night he was in great form. On a break between films, away from Colonel Parker, free of pressures and responsibilities, he could relax and play.

On the way to Vegas we all listened to music, nibbled on snacks, and drank Pepsis. In the front seat, Elvis and Gene joked in their own language. Elvis would say something and Gene would reply with a complete non sequitur. When conversation lagged, they engaged in surprise attacks, punching each other. If Gene thought he'd landed a good one, he'd take off running toward the back of the bus, aware that Elvis could always pull over and chase him.

These antics continued throughout most of the exhausting drive across the desert. I felt out of sync with the private jokes and crazy high jinks. It was quite obvious that the boys picked up on Elvis's every mood. I did not yet fit in.

We arrived in Las Vegas around seven in the morning. I was tired and falling asleep when Elvis called out, "We're comin' into Vegas. Look around—all you see is hotels. It's called Sin City. Isn't that right, Smiff?" Gene mumbled one of his silly replies and Elvis laughed as usual.

The Strip looked quiet. There were a lot of taxis, some cars, and a few tired people strolling along the streets. I noticed it was extremely hot for 7 A.M., especially since it was only June.

We checked into the Sahara Hotel and to my amazement, despite the early hour, people were everywhere. Elvis pointed to the casino, noisy with the rhythmic sounds of the slot machines, the sporadic ringing of bells, and an occasional yell from the craps tables.

"Is this normal?" I asked Elvis.

"Honey, you ain't seen nothin' yet. Wait till tonight," he replied.

That wouldn't be easy. Despite being tired, I stood fascinated, watching the gamblers clustered at the various tables and the slot machines. Elvis took my arm. "Come on, Baby. Let's go up to the room. There'll be plenty of time for this later. We better get some rest."

We followed the bellboy to the suite, and the entourage efficiently began arranging the rooms to Elvis's liking. They unpacked his clothes, placing them neatly in his closet, lining up his shoes by color, and setting out his toiletries in the bathroom. In the living room, they set up his record player and speakers, lowered the lights to create the right atmosphere, and turned on all the television sets.

"Why do you always have the TV on?" I asked Elvis.

"It keeps me company," he said. "When it's on, I feel like there are people around."

He despised entering a quiet room, and soon I too adopted the habit of automatically turning on the TV whenever I walked into a room.

An hour later the assistants had the suite looking lived in, with everything in its proper place. Elvis said good night to the boys and cautioned them not to wake us too early. He locked the bedroom door and got undressed and into bed. As I climbed in beside him, I noticed that he was taking a number of prescribed sleeping pills, but I didn't pay much attention to them. I wasn't knowledgeable enough even to suspect any potential threat.

I lay there blissfully happy: Finally we were able to spend an entire night sleeping together.

Elvis was looking at me. "Do you believe this, Baby? After all this time, here you are. Who'd ever have thought we'd pull this off? Let's not even think about you going back. We'll have a good time. We'll think about the other when the time comes."

His words were starting to slur. His reactions slowed down. He pulled me closer and told me, again and again, "I'm glad you're here . . ." And then—silence. I looked over at the bottles of pills near the bed and realized I still had competition.

9

WHEN I AWOKE the next afternoon, I looked over at Elvis and snuggled against him as closely as I could. He put his arms around me, holding me as he slept. I studied his eyebrows, his long black eyelashes, his perfect nose, and his beautiful, full mouth. After a while I ached from lying in the same position but I didn't move; it might wake him.

I thought about the pills he had taken earlier. They mystified me but I felt Elvis must know what was best for him and I decided to put the matter out of my mind.

He must have sensed that I was staring at him; he suddenly opened his eyes and started to laugh. "What are you doing? If I didn't know any better, I'd think you were putting a hex on me."

"I couldn't sleep," I said, embarrassed that he'd caught me studying him. "I guess I'm too excited."

Sitting up, he said, "Well, Little Girl, the first thing I need is a cup of black coffee. Press number four on the intercom and tell Billy to order us some breakfast. He knows what I like and just tell him what you want. Tell him to have it here in half an hour and to make sure the coffee's hot."

Getting out of bed, he flipped on the TV and walked into the bathroom. A moment later he stuck out his head and grinned. "Get dressed, Little One, I want to show you off a little."

That was all I needed to hear. I jumped out of bed and ran into my bathroom to get ready. As I dressed in a casual summer outfit I could hear music coming from the living room. I cracked open the adjoining door and was surprised to see all the boys up and dressed, with breakfast set up on the dining-room table.

I finished combing my hair and walked out to the living room, where the guys greeted me with friendly smiles and hellos. Elvis wasn't there yet, so no one had begun eating. Everyone was pretty quiet. Although it was after four in the afternoon, it seemed like early morning.

About fifteen minutes later, Elvis came into the room, all dressed up in a three-piece suit, and I realized that nothing in my wardrobe was suitable. He walked over to the stereo and put on his latest record, saying he'd just finished a recording session and wanted me to hear the songs. Then we all sat down for breakfast.

It was fun hearing his recordings before they were released to the public. He asked me what I thought of each song, and since I knew what the kids back in Europe were listening to, I felt my comments might be helpful. At least I wanted to believe they were. "I really like the fast-paced ones," I said, "like 'Jailhouse Rock.' Why don't you record more songs like that? These don't seem as much like rock and roll as your earlier records."

Elvis shot me a look of such pure disgust that I was petrified. "Goddamn it," he snapped. "I didn't ask for your opinion on what style I should sing. I asked if you like the songs, that's all—yes or no. I get enough amateur opinions as it is. I don't need another one." He got up and stalked into the bedroom and slammed the door. Trying to regain my composure, I fought back tears. I was embarrassed and confused. What was wrong with what I'd said? How could that upset him so?

Luckily, the boys had already left the table and were all doing odd jobs or were in another room. I didn't know if any of them had heard Elvis's tirade, but I didn't want to face them. I knew Elvis had a temper—I had witnessed it in Germany—but never before had he directed it at me.

Slowly I rose from the table, wondering where to go. Elvis's bedroom door was still tightly shut and, although I was sharing his room, I hesitated to go in for fear he'd start yelling. Not knowing what else to do, I sat down next to the albums and started going through them, pretending to look interested. Soon I heard the bedroom door open and saw Elvis standing in the doorway. He motioned to me to come over. Reluctantly, I put back the records and walked into the room, fearful of what he was going to say. He closed the door, sat me down on the edge of the bed, and—to my surprise—began to apologize: "I'm sorry, Baby. What happened before really had nothing to do with you. I just finished that recording session and it's pretty damn good compared to what they usually want me to do for these movies."

He talked more about his last film, the story line, the songs, the dialogue, all of which he thought were inane.

I was beginning to understand some of his frustrations and dissatisfaction. I remembered our talks in Germany. Elvis had been proud of his film accomplishments before entering the Army. He had talked hopefully about doing movies with more substance and fewer songs.

"Cilla, from now on I plan to keep my singing career and my acting career strictly separate." He believed he was capable of performing more demanding roles than he was getting, and to prepare himself, he still studied certain actors whom he admired, such as James Dean in *Giant* and Marlon Brando in *On the Waterfront* and *The Wild One.*

"But I keep getting offered the same musicals, same story lines," he complained, "and they're getting worse and worse."

His biggest problem was that these films and their soundtrack albums were always huge hits.

Shaking off his serious mood, he grabbed my hand and said, "Come on, Baby, we're goin' shopping." This was Elvis's way of making up for his outburst, but it took me a little while to get over it. Forcing an enthusiastic smile,

I went along. I was beginning to understand how everyone's mood played off Elvis.

Taking Gene and Alan with us, we jumped into a waiting limo and rode around until Elvis spotted a boutique where glamorous gowns made of sequins, lace, and frills graced the beautiful mannequins in the window. He called out to the driver, "Let's stop here."

Taking my hand, he led me inside, followed by the entire entourage, surely the most unlikely band of characters ever to invade an elegant dress shop. The salesgirl was speechless.

"Hello, ma'am. I'm Elvis Presley and we're just looking around. Maybe you could show us something that might interest my little friend over there."

They both looked over at me. The look on the clerk's face told me we were thinking the same thing: These clothes were far too sophisticated for such a young girl. But when Elvis saw something he liked, he didn't think in terms of age. While the saleswoman went to the back to rummage around for whatever she had in sizes six and four, Elvis was rifling through the racks, pulling out a number of dazzling creations, asking me which ones I liked.

"They're all beautiful," I said. "I just don't know how I'd look in them."

"You let me be the judge of that," he said, winking at Gene, who mumbled one of his non sequiturs. We all dissolved into fits of laughter that brought the shopgirl rushing back with a huge selection of dresses. Elvis designated his preferences and said, "Try them on. And pick out any others you like."

Thrilled, I chose a half-dozen gowns with matching shoes and headed for the dressing room. The salesgirl followed. Away from Elvis's eyes she treated me like a little kid, but I was so enchanted with the clothes that I didn't care.

As I posed in front of the mirror in a long black jersey gown and a pair of gold high-heeled sandals, I hardly recognized myself. I definitely appeared older, very sexy and very sophisticated.

As I stepped out of the dressing room, the salesgirl mumbled, "Not bad for a kid." Elvis took one look and said, "Hot damn, we'll take it."

We stayed for over two hours, while Elvis bought me not only the black sheath, but also a midnight blue satin, several lovely silks and chiffons, and a beautiful baby-blue brocade gown, all accented by matching capes and bags and shoes.

When we left the shop we found a crowd had gathered. Elvis glanced at Alan, who immediately disappeared. Then he gave a number of people his autograph, said goodbye, and Gene quickly led us through the back of the shop and out the door, where Alan was waiting with the car ready to take us to the hotel.

Back at our suite, Elvis said, "I'm hungry. Joe, order me a steak, but make sure you tell them well done. What do you want, Honey?"

"Hell, E," Joe said, "I always tell them well done."

"Well, tell them again," Elvis shot back. "I'll be god-damned if it doesn't always come back half raw."

To Elvis, raw was slightly pink. Everyone specified "burnt" when ordering for him.

Elvis turned to Alan and said, "Hog Ears" (he had pet names for all his employees), "make arrangements for Red Skelton's midnight show, and see if there's anyone in the hotel who can do Cilla's hair and makeup."

"Hair and makeup?" I said. "What's wrong with my hair?"

It was long and dark brown, casually combed. But beyond feeling he didn't like my hair, now I began to think he didn't like my looks.

"There's nothing wrong with it, honey. It's just that this is Las Vegas. Everyone has their hair done. You need to apply more makeup around your eyes. Make them stand out more. They're too plain naturally. I like a lot of makeup. It defines your features."

Defines your features? At that time it made a lot of sense—and Elvis knew best.

While we waited for dinner, Elvis put one of his records on the stereo and sat next to me, singing along with his own voice on the record. In that moment I fell in love all over again. When he sang about lost love or a life lived out in grief and pain, he delivered the lyrics with such conviction that I'd feel the hurt. He'd been a fan of country music since long before it became popular and was always impressed by the raw emotion in those recordings.

After dinner we got ready for the evening. At Elvis's request, Armond, a hairdresser at the hotel, came in and spent nearly two hours creating my new look. He teased and twisted up my hair with one long curl falling in front of my left shoulder. Then he applied my makeup so heavily that you couldn't tell if my eyes were black, blue, or black and blue. It was that look of the sixties, only more extreme. That was what Elvis wanted.

When I put on my brand-new brocade gown, my transformation from an innocent sixteen-year-old to a sophisticated siren was complete. I looked like one of the lead dancers in the Folies-Bergère.

"Goddamn, what happened to Little Cilla," Elvis said when he saw me. "You look beautiful. Joe, come here. Look what I found."

Joe walked in and did a double take.

"Sure doesn't look like the same girl we met in Germany, wearing a sailor dress," Joe said.

Everyone laughed, and we left to see Red Skelton's midnight show.

We arrived just after the lights went down, and the maître d', using a flashlight, quickly led us to our table. Elvis always tried to arrive unnoticed so he wouldn't distract attention from the headlining star. But word always spread throughout the audience that he was there and within a few seconds, the whispering would start and heads would turn.

At the end of a show Elvis would try to exit just before the house lights went up, but on that night we didn't make it. The lights came on and suddenly we were surrounded by an enthusiastic crowd of people pushing and shoving, hoping to get an autograph.

Being just under five foot four, I was engulfed in the

crush and I began to feel faint. I reached out for Elvis as I started to panic and said, "I can't breathe. I have to get out."

At first he grinned, then his look turned to concern as he saw my desperation. Still smiling and signing autographs, he said to Alan, "Get Cilla out quick. I'll be along as soon as I can."

Alan took one look at me, grabbed my hand, and pushed his way through the crowd, out of the hotel. Once in the fresh air, I regained my composure. From that experience I learned to scout out the exits whenever Elvis and I entered a crowded room.

When we came out a few minutes later, like clockwork, the limo was waiting. We jumped in and sped off to the Sahara Hotel for my first adventure in gambling. Elvis wasn't a serious player—it didn't matter if he won or lost. He played for the fun of it. A cigar jutting impressively from his mouth, a drink in one hand, and his eyes squinting suspiciously at the cards, he gave a flawless impersonation of Clark Gable as Rhett Butler. I sat proudly beside him, his very own Scarlett O'Hara.

I'd never played blackjack before, but after a few hands, Elvis thought I had the hang of it. He handed me five hundred dollars and jokingly said, "You're on your own, kid. What you win is yours, and what you lose . . . well, we'll have to discuss that later."

I smiled and called for the dealer to include me in the game. I looked at my hand, counting on my fingers under the table. *Nine plus eight is seventeen, then a five makes . . .*

"Twenty-one!" I shouted. Throwing down my cards, I looked over to Elvis for his approval.

"Let's see," he said, slowly scooping up the cards. Squinting one eye, he counted them. Then, leaning over to me, he grinned and whispered, "Sorry, Baby. It's twenty-two."

I was so embarrassed that I excused myself and took refuge in the ladies' room. When I gathered up the courage to return, I tried again, and luckily ended up winning two hundred dollars.

For the next two weeks, we slept during the day and played at night. If there was a show, we saw it; if there was a casino, we played it. To help me adapt to this fast-paced life-style and unusual hours I would join Elvis and the others in taking amphetamines and sleeping pills. Despite whatever misgivings I had about pills, I took them. In order for me to keep up, they became essential.

I was adapting. My inhibitions were dropping away and I became more assertive, especially after taking the pills. I liked the feeling. Even though it was an escape from reality, we were in sync and to me I was fitting more into his world. We were learning all about each other and using this trip to make up for the two years we had been apart. Both of us were falling more in love—and avoiding any thought of the moment when we'd have to part again.

10

THE DAY BEFORE I was to leave for Germany, Elvis took me aside and said, "Baby, as much as I hate to say it, we're gonna have to face it. Our time is up." I broke down and hung onto him tightly, burying my head in his chest.

"I'm not leaving," I said, sobbing. "I'm not leaving you. I'll call my parents and say I missed the plane."

"C'mon, Baby. You think they're gonna fall for that?"

"Then I'll tell them the truth: that I love you and that I won't come back."

"Hey, hey." He was trying to calm me. "You're just gonna make it worse for the next time. I've been thinkin', I always wanted you to see Graceland. But right now, I've got some business to take care of in Memphis for a few weeks, and then I've gotta do another film. So if you go back and do well in school and behave yourself, maybe your parents will let you spend Christmas at Graceland with me and my family."

I loved the idea, but Christmas was six months away. Anything could happen between now and then.

That night in bed Elvis held me very close for a long time. I felt that he was doing more than just comforting me. He was telling me how deeply he cared.

And more than that: His deep belief in consummating our love affair only in marriage gave me hope for the future.

Later, our lovemaking had more feeling and intensity than ever before. Elvis wasn't going to let me go home without my taking a little of him with me. He didn't enter me; he didn't have to. He fulfilled my every desire.

"I want you back the way you are now," he whispered just before dawn. "And remember, I'll always know."

I smiled and nodded. I couldn't conceive of wanting anyone but him.

Elvis didn't walk me into the airport. We kissed goodbye in the limousine. It was a tender but excruciatingly brief moment. I didn't think the pain could have been greater even if he told me I'd never return.

I walked onto the plane like a robot. I was in a daze that lasted throughout the eleven-hour flight. I talked to no one and didn't care who saw the tears constantly streaming down my face. My world had come to an abrupt end. Finally I closed my eyes and in my mind I relived every moment of my visit. Suddenly the stewardess was telling us to fasten our seat belts for the landing. The thought of freshening up before we arrived never occurred to me. I just sat in a daze, waiting for the plane to taxi to a stop. Then I listlessly gathered up my things and made my way out.

When I first saw my parents, my mother was crying with joy at seeing me and my father was wearing a big welcome-home smile. But as I came nearer, their expressions changed from delight to absolute horror. My father turned away angrily. For a moment my mother just stared. Then she reached into her purse, pulled out a mirror, and thrust it at me.

"Look at yourself! How could you walk off the plane like that?"

I glanced at myself in the mirror and immediately understood their response. Two weeks before, I had left them, a fresh-faced sixteen-year-old, wearing a suitable white cotton suit and innocent of anything but a touch of mascara. Now, not only was I wearing the heavy makeup that Elvis liked, but my tears had smeared it all over my face. I hadn't bothered to lift a comb to my hair, which was unkempt and tangled. My parents were shocked and disappointed.

Too embarrassed to look at them, I put my hand to my face and nonchalantly tried to wipe off the residue of black mascara and liner. Then I said, 'I'd like to go to the ladies' room."

"You're going straight home," my father snapped. "If you left it on this long, you might as well keep it on another hour." He hardly said another word to me until we got home and I washed my face.

Christmas in the Beaulieu family was always a major production, but Christmas 1962 was one time I wasn't concerned about presents. I was bound for the place that I had often dreamed about but never let myself believe that I would actually see—Graceland.

Getting there hadn't been easy. The plotting and scheming had started one morning at 2:10 A.M., when I had sleepily answered the phone to hear Elvis's voice. He seemed in great spirits. Laughing and joking, he told me that RCA had sent him some horrible demo records for his next movie. "I'm listening to 'em, Baby, and I can't believe what I'm hearing. I have to laugh because if I don't, I'll start cryin'."

I chuckled sympathetically, but I could hear the sadness in his voice. Then he said softly, "Little Girl, I want you here for Christmas. I don't care how you arrange it or what you have to tell your parents. I'll go along with anything you say, as long as you get here."

I was shaking as I hung up the phone. I couldn't imagine my parents allowing me to leave again—especially at Christmas—but there was no way I was going to let him down.

After a few days of silently avoiding the subject, I casually brought up Elvis's request to my mother.

"Absolutely not," she declared. "It's out of the question. Christmas is for the family. That's the way it's always been and it's not going to change—not even for Elvis Presley."

I wouldn't give up. My poor mother was torn between making a dream come true for her daughter and doing what was right as a parent.

"When will this end?" she murmured with an anguished expression. Finally she agreed to speak to my father.

That was the breakthrough.

Again the pleas. Again the promises.

One month later, I was on a flight bound for the United States. Elvis had asked Vernon and Dee to meet me at La Guardia Airport in New York and escort me to Memphis because he didn't want me to travel alone.

By the time we reached Memphis, I was both exhausted and exhilarated. We went to Vernon's home on Hermitage Drive, a short distance from Graceland. Elvis had left explicit instructions that only he could drive me through the gates of Graceland.

A few minutes after we arrived, he called. His father handed me the phone. Before I could say two words, Elvis blurted he was on his way. Minutes later the door flew open and I was in his arms.

Graceland was everything Elvis had said it would be. The front lawn was adorned with a nativity scene and the white columns of the mansion were ablaze with holiday lights. It was one of the most beautiful sights I'd ever laid eyes on.

Inside the mansion a crowd of Elvis's friends and relatives all stood waiting to greet me. I felt relaxed and comfortable as he introduced me to everyone, because I had already met several of his friends when I was in Los Angeles.

Then Elvis said, "Cilla, there's someone special who's waiting for you." With a smile, he led me up the stairs and opened the door to his grandmother's room.

"Dodger," he called out. "Look who's here. It's little Cilla. She's come a long way, Dodger, to be with little us."

Using endearing terms like "little us" was his way of being affectionate. His mother had raised him on this sweet talk and Elvis spoke it with those he cherished. Feet, for instance, were "sooties"; milk, "butch"; teeth, "toophies"; love, "yuv"; little, "yittle." In moments of intimacy he would switch to third-person address: Him yuvs you and her yuvs him.

Dodger smiled and greeted me in her soft voice. "Good God, child, it took you a long time to get here."

She was sitting in a high-backed overstuffed chair. I leaned over and she gave me a hug and patted me on the back. I was delighted at how good Dodger was looking, her hair, once completely gray, was now a natural-looking dark brown. I noticed she wasn't as thin as she'd been in Germany. At 14 Goethestrasse Dodger had presided over a busy household; at Graceland she had withdrawn to her room.

After Elvis left us alone, I could tell something was bothering her and asked, "Grandma, how has everything been with you?" She looked at me and then down at the lace handkerchief in her lap.

"I don't know, Hon. I'm worried about Elvis and

Me at two.
Me at thirteen.
Who would ever guess?

Elvis rocking and rolling in 1956. UPI/Bettmann Newsphotos

Rehearsing for The Ed Sullivan Show, 1956. UPI/Bettmann Newsphotos

Loving You, 1957. AP/Wide World
Photos

Jailhouse Rock, 1957. Springer
Bettmann Film Archive

King Creole, 1958. Springer/Bettmann Film Archive

14 Goethestrasse, where Elvis and I first met. James Whitmore, Life Magazine © Time Inc.

Me and Grandma Presley. James Whitmore, Life Magazine © Time Inc

Paul and Ann Beaulieu, my parents.

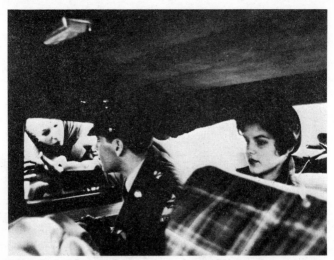

When Elvis left Germany to return to the States...James Whitmore; Life Magazine © Time Inc.

I accompanied him to the airport...James Whitmore, Life Magazine © Time Inc.

He told me to wave so he could spot me in the crowd...James Whitmore, Life Magazine © Time Inc.

As promised, he turned to look for me...James Whitmore, Life Magazine © Time Inc.

and wave goodbye ...James Whitmore, Life Magazine © Time Inc.

The moment of truth: Suddenly Elvis was gone... James Whitmore, Life Magazine © Time Inc.

and I was escorted away. James Whitmore, Life Magazine © Time Inc.

Graceland. UPI/Bettmann Newsphotos

Elvis bulldozing a house behind Graceland.

The way Elvis liked me. Blue Light Studios, Memphis, Tennessee

Elvis behind the wheel, me in the center, Charlie Hodge, and Joe Esposito headed for California—our last trip by bus!

Me and Honey, 1963.

My first car. Elvis gave me this Corvair for graduation.

With Ann-Margret in Viva Las Vegas, 1963. UPI/Bettmann Newsphotos

Me and Domino, 1967.

Elvis and his Tennessee walking horse, Bear.

Elvis and me in Palm Springs, toasting each other the night before our wedding.

The wedding breakfast in Las Vegas, 1967. AP/Wide World Photos

Mrs. Elvis Presley. It had a different sound, a nicer ring than "lover" or "live-in Lolita." AP/Wide World Photos

Our wedding day.

Vernon. Elvis is still upset over his Daddy's marriage."
Vernon and Dee had gotten married a year earlier. "He
don't spend much time at Graceland anymore and his
Daddy's worried. I hate to see the two of 'em upset like
that. Lord have mercy. Elvis didn't go to the weddin',
you know. Elvis is tryin' hard, but when she comes over
he just gets up and leaves the room. I don't know if he'll
ever accept it."

She reached for her snuffbox. It was an endearing
habit that she tried to keep secret.

"But I don't want you to go worrying about it," she
continued. "You go off and have a good time with Elvis.
That young'un needs you now."

I nodded and kissed her cheek. "I promise I'll take care
of him, Dodger," I said, feeling guilty leaving her. She
worried too much, just as all the Presleys did. It was
contagious.

She laughed softly and said with a smile, "Ain't no
one ever called me that but Elvis."

All that night, the guys played pool, watched TV, and
hung around the kitchen badgering Alberta ("VO5")
while she played short-order cook.

I realized that there was no set routine at Graceland.
Everyone came and went as they pleased. It wasn't a
home, but rather an open house, available to the guys
and their dates—all with Elvis's approval, of course.

The evening ended around 4 A.M., when Elvis finally

said good night to everyone and took my hand. I was really exhausted since, in anticipation of the trip, I hadn't slept for two days. As I walked up the white-carpeted staircase, I closed my eyes and wished I was already in bed.

In his room, Elvis gave me two large red pills, explaining, "Take these now, and by the time you come to bed, you'll be nice and relaxed." I really didn't need anything, but he insisted, saying that they would help me sleep better and were a little stronger than what I'd taken before.

I didn't recognize them. They were larger than I'd ever taken before. You'd have to be a horse to get these down, I thought, but I reluctantly swallowed them.

I went into the dressing room to bathe, and as I sank into the tub, my head settled on the edge. My arm was so heavy I could barely raise my hand; my eyelids seemed weighted. But I felt good and kind of silly.

The longer I soaked, the less energy I had and I only barely managed to get out of the tub. Trying to focus on the bed, I staggered over to where Elvis was lying. Then I collapsed.

After that, I was occasionally awakened by the sound of distant voices. One time, I thought I saw Elvis whispering to me. Another time I saw his father. I didn't know if I was dreaming or hallucinating, but when I closed my eyes I could feel the room spinning around.

Then I felt a soft hand gently rubbing and patting my arm. "Priscilla? Priscilla? Hon, it's Grandma, you all right?" Slowly I tried to lift my head, but it was too heavy and it fell back down.

"What'd you give this young'un?" I heard someone say. "You got no business givin' her something she's not used to. Son, maybe we ought to call a doctor. She's in bad shape. I don't think we should take any chances."

I managed to focus my half-closed eyes on Elvis and gave him a wink and a giddy grin.

He said, "Hell no, we're not callin' any doctor. Look, she's comin' to."

Kneeling beside me, he held up my head, and I saw that I wasn't in his room but lying on the white chaise lounge in his office, which adjoined the bedroom.

"What am I doing here?"

"I walked you in here after the first day," he answered in a concerned tone. "We were trying to revive you."

"But I just went to bed," I said, slurring my words.

"Baby, you had us all scared. You've been out for two days on two goddamn five-hundred-milligram Placidyls. Must have been out of my head giving them to you that way."

"Two days! That's two days off my trip. What's today?"

"December twenty-third."

"Oh no."

"Don't worry. We still have plenty of time." He smiled at me and said, "I promise, Baby, I'll make it up to you."

11

"MERRY CHRISTMAS," Elvis said proudly, handing me a honey-colored six-week-old puppy.

"Oh, Elvis. He's the cutest thing I've ever seen, and the smallest." I gave Elvis a big hug and heard a muffled yelp between us. "Oh, *Honey!*" I said. "I'm sorry." I had unwittingly just christened the pup Honey.

It was Christmas Eve. Elvis had prayed for a white Christmas and—as if on cue—that night three full inches of snow fell.

The gathering around the tree included Vernon and Dee, her three sons—David, Ricky, and Billy—the entourage and their wives, and a handful of Elvis's other relatives and friends. Everyone was pleasant and made me feel welcome, though it must have seemed strange to see me rather than Anita sitting beside Elvis. Anita had shared Christmas with him the two previous years. Sometimes I couldn't help wondering if he missed her. It wasn't easy for him to let go of people. I knew that.

It was fun watching Elvis open gifts. "Just what I needed, another jewelry box," he quipped, unwrapping the fourth one of the evening. He looked over at Gene Smith, one of the few people who could consistently make Elvis laugh.

"You give me this, Gene?" he asked.

Gene mumbled, "Naw, E, I didn't give it to you."

Then Elvis reconsidered. "On second thought, I don't guess you did, Gene. It's got too much taste."

"Ah, E, how can you say that?" Gene was mumbling in his slow Southern drawl.

"Easy." Elvis's eyes narrowed. "Just look at you, Gene, a living example of ba-a-a-d taste."

Pretending to be insulted, Gene walked away scratching his head, as everyone laughed.

Although there were lots of jokes, I sensed a sadness in Elvis's look as our eyes met, and I couldn't help recalling what he'd once said to me in Germany: "Christmas just won't be the same at Graceland without Mama. It'll be hard for me, and I don't know if I can bear the loneliness. But I guess I'll manage. God will give me the strength somehow."

"Oh, look, Elvis," I said, trying to distract him with a large, colorfully wrapped present. "Here's one more you forgot to open." It was my own gift to him, a musical cigarette case, which I'd purposely saved for last. I held my breath as he unwrapped it.

He opened the box and it began to play "Love Me Tender."

"I love it! I really do, Cilla. Thank you."

There was a twinkle in his eyes, and I wished I could always make him this happy.

After Christmas we did something exciting every night, usually beginning after midnight. Sometimes Elvis rented either the Memphian or the Malco theater to watch movies. Other times he rented the entire Rainbow Skating Rink, the infamous roller rink I'd heard so much about.

My first night there I was lacing up my skates when the boys asked me, "Do you know how to skate?"

"Sure," I said.

"But do you know *how* to skate?" they persisted.

I got the message real fast when a box of knee pads was passed around. This was not your ordinary around-the-rink-to-organ-music skating. The idea here was to keep your bones intact.

I wobbled onto the rink only to wobble off. I wasn't about to stay on that floor after seeing the determined looks on the other skaters' faces. They made the Roller Derby look mild. From the sideline, I watched them rounding the rink, adjusting their jackets and shirts so they weren't too tight and checking that their arms and legs were securely padded.

Then Elvis skated into their midst, calling out, "Okay, everybody. Y'all clear the way on the sidelines. I don't want anybody hurt over there. Honey, why don't you get on the other side there with Louise [Gene Smith's wife]. The rest of you, get your asses somewhere else." They all started laughing, and he said, "Okay, let's go!"

About twenty-five skaters locked hands, forming what they called a whip. Skating abreast, they began circling the rink, building up speed. The object of the game was to remain unscathed at speeds of over ten miles per hour. It could be very dangerous if you were to lose your balance or if you were at the tail end, when, by turning quickly, they all "cracked the whip."

There were a lot of falls, but despite the danger, Elvis seemed to know exactly what he was doing. I noticed that whenever someone was hurt, he was the first to see if they were all right and to decide if they should continue to play.

I still don't know how anybody kept from getting seriously injured, yet no one complained and most of them were even willing to do it again the next night. It was rough, but as Elvis put it, "If you're man enough to get out there, then you better be man enough to take the licks."

New Year's Eve was approaching. Elvis told Alan to rent the Manhattan Club for the evening and to invite about two hundred people, Elvis's friends and the presidents and other members of his fan clubs.

Although I was excited about the party, I couldn't help thinking that after New Year's Eve I would have to leave. Elvis kept telling me not to think about it. I noticed that whenever I mentioned a problem to him he'd just say, "It'll all work out, don't worry about it. I've got enough to think about without having to worry about that."

He always avoided problems. If I was disturbed or depressed, or if I felt we were becoming distant and wanted to get closer by talking it out, he avoided me or told me my timing was bad. There was never a good time.

Once I reproached him about the attention he was lavishing on the girlfriend of one of the regulars. She was very attractive, about my height, with black hair and a nice figure. She had come into the kitchen, where several of us were sitting, and Elvis, who was wearing dark sunglasses, began making comments like, "Boy, it's getting warm in here. Anybody else warm?"

I was so upset I left the room. I waited for him to go upstairs, then followed shortly behind him. "Elvis, I have to talk to you," I said.

"Sure, Honey, what is it?"

"I saw the way you were eyeing that girl. It upset me."

"Look, woman," he said, losing his temper. "No one tells me who I can look at and who I can't. Besides, your imagination's getting carried away. I've seen her ass around here long before today."

With that I stomped out, slamming the bedroom door. I felt betrayed that he'd even desire another woman and was annoyed that he'd never admit it. I became obsessed and watched what Elvis liked, what attracted him, trying to be everything he ever imagined a woman could be, and more.

The New Year's Eve party at the Manhattan Club started around 10 P.M., but Elvis timed our arrival a few minutes before midnight. We just had time to order double screwdrivers when the countdown began. Then we all sang "Auld Lang Syne."

As people shouted "Happy New Year!" Elvis pulled me close and said, "Baby, I don't want you to go back. You're staying here. We'll call your parents in the morning."

I was in such a state of ecstasy that I didn't notice what I was drinking: four double screwdrivers, all drunk through a straw. After one double, I was feeling high; after four, I was reeling. I went into the ladies' room with Louise and stayed there for what seemed like hours, swaying back and forth in the stall, trying to get myself together.

When we finally returned to the table, I tried to act as if everything was okay, but Elvis took one look at me and said, "Baby, we better get you home. You're in no condition to be here." He asked his old friend George Klein, the Memphis disc jockey, if he would take me home.

I spent most of the ride back to Graceland with my head out the window. George and his date walked me to the door, where we said good night, and I let myself in.

Gripping the banister, I slowly climbed the white stairs, shedding my clothing as I went—my jacket, purse, shoes, and blouse left in a long trail up the steps. By the time I reached the bedroom I was wearing only my bra and panties. I collapsed on the bed and passed out.

A few hours later I heard Elvis tiptoe into the room and come over to me. His condition was not much better than mine. I could make out his silhouette against the ceiling above me. I didn't stir. Gently, he took off the rest of my clothes. Then he kissed me and kissed me over and over. This night we almost went too far. His vow was nearly broken. My passion had gotten to him and under the influence of alcohol, he weakened. Then, before I knew what happened, he withdrew saying, "No. Not like this." It had to be special, just as he'd always planned.

I have to admit that, at that moment, I didn't care if it was special and I didn't care what he'd vowed. I didn't care, in fact, what *he* wanted at all. I only knew I wanted him.

The next morning my head throbbed with a terrible hangover. I felt ashamed and embarrassed—and yet not at all sorry about what we'd done. He was a little closer to being all mine.

The moment of truth came when we called my father in Germany. Elvis was on the extension in his office and I was on another phone somewhere else in the house. Though the connection to Wiesbaden was filled with static, there was no mistaking my father's words.

"Young lady, I will not go through this conversation again. We made an agreement. You were to leave there on the second of January. You've got one day left and you'd better be on that flight!"

Elvis interjected, "Captain, sir, if she could just stay a couple more days. I have to be back in L.A. soon, and it would be nice—"

"Elvis, I can't do that. She has to be back in school and that was the deal. I'm sorry. Priscilla Ann, are you there?"

"Yes," I answered.

"We'll be at the airport. You know the time; we'll see you then."

I was furious. I flew into Elvis's office where, sitting behind his desk, he was just hanging up.

"I hate them. I hate them both," I yelled like a spoiled child. "Why are they stopping us? They just want me home to babysit, to take care of the kids, that's all."

Elvis's face was flushed with anger. "We made a goddamn agreement—who the hell does he think he is, talking like that on the goddamn phone—him and his military upbringing."

He grabbed the phone and called down to the kitchen, demanding, "Where's my daddy! He down there? Tell him to come upstairs to the office."

Within seconds Vernon was at the door. "What is it, Son?"

"Goddamn Captain Beaulieu," he shouted. "We just called to see if Cilla could stay a few more days and he comes off with this cocky attitude and refuses with his jargon about making agreements."

"Now calm down, Son. It ain't that bad. He was probably just concerned about her being home in time for school."

"School, what the hell do I care about school?" Elvis snapped, ignoring Vernon's efforts to soothe him. "Put her into school here, that'll solve everything. She doesn't need school. Hell, they don't teach you anything nowadays anyway."

"Well, Son, she's gonna have to go back, there ain't no two ways about it, give or take a day or two."

"Goddamn, Daddy, you're not helpin' matters any," Elvis said, but he was beginning to calm down. He sat back in his big desk chair and swiveled it around to face the window, then gazed out toward the pastures. Finally he turned around and announced that he had a plan.

Elvis's strategy called for me to return to Germany and to arrive in good spirits, then to concentrate on doing well in school so that my parents wouldn't be able to use my poor grades as an excuse for not letting me return. Elvis wanted me to finish high school in Memphis and to that end he would make arrangements for me to return as soon as possible.

12

ALTHOUGH ELVIS SAID that I should greet my parents with a friendly smile, from the moment I got off the plane, my attitude was one of defiance. I now believed that my parents were a threat to my future happiness. I didn't realize that their fears and concerns were entirely reasonable. All that mattered to me was what Elvis and I wanted, and no one was going to stand in our way.

The weather was cold and dreary, which certainly didn't help my mood. I walked through customs to find my parents waiting. Noting my attitude, their expressions were cool, their welcome stiff. No loving arms wrapped around me, no loving words greeted me. Only my father's abrupt order, "Let's go."

The drive back to Wiesbaden seemed longer than

forty-five minutes. I sat in the backseat in icy silence. No one mentioned my request to stay at Graceland.

"All in all, did you have a nice time?" Dad ventured.

"Yes," I replied, looking out the window at the clusters of trees bare from the harsh winter.

"Did Elvis like your present?" Mother asked hopefully.

"Yes," I assured her. "He loved it."

"Was it as cold in Memphis as it gets here?" Dad asked, keeping the conversation light, trying to make me open up and talk.

"No, it's colder here," I replied sharply, referring to both the weather and my attitude. Our eyes met in the rearview mirror and surprisingly, Dad looked away rather than reacting to my cutting remark.

I knew I was pushing my luck with them, but I couldn't suppress my feelings and pretend that everything was all right. I was so deeply in love that chitchat seemed pointless—as did everything *except* for Elvis. I remembered how he had held me before we said good-bye, with such emotion and need that nothing could keep me away from him. How could I explain these adult feelings to my parents who, I thought, could never understand and would think me silly or just infatuated?

When we arrived home Dad said, "Well, you've got school tomorrow, so try to get as much rest as you can tonight."

Mom added, "You should have dinner and get right to bed."

Did they both honestly think that I could slip back into the routine of ordinary life?

I rebelled against going to school. I skipped classes, went to town, and downed a few beers with whomever I could get to join me. My attitude worsened along with my grades.

My parents were as confused as any caring parents would be, hoping the problem would eventually go away. But I didn't make it easy for them. What had started out as a simple introduction to the world's greatest rock-and-roll star had turned into a nightmare for them.

Elvis began calling me almost immediately, and we'd talk for hours. My parents heard me whispering and giggling till three in the morning and wondered what on earth we could be talking about for so long. Nothing really—yet it seemed like everything.

I began to reveal to my mother that Elvis and I loved each other and longed to be together. Finally one day I summoned the courage to tell her that Elvis wanted me to finish school in Memphis. Her response: an unqualified no. She felt it could wait until my father's tour of duty was over. That would be the end of summer, she said, and there was no need for me to return to Elvis sooner.

"But Mother," I pleaded, "you don't understand. He wants me there with him."

"Why you?" she asked, her voice thick with emotion. "Why can't he find someone his own age? You're only sixteen.   What is this man doing to our family?"

She buried her face in her hands and began crying.

I did feel sorry for her. We were always close, she was always there for me, but this time she just didn't understand. I hated seeing her in pain, but nothing seemed more important to me than Elvis. Not even my mother.

"He's not anything like you imagine," I said, "and he needs me, Mother. I won't get hurt. Please talk to Dad."

Slowly she raised her head and looked at me.

"Cilla, I'd never forgive myself if I let you go and if you came back to us with a broken heart. You're so young! You have no idea what lies ahead of you. All you know is you're in love. Do you know how difficult that is to fight?" She sighed. "I wouldn't wish this on any parent."

She brushed away her tears and after a moment said, "All right, I'll talk to your father, but not just yet. It's still too soon."

I gave her a big hug and whispered, "Thank you, Mother. I know you can do it. I love you."

Now I had to wait for my mother to intercede. I knew how much my father was against the idea. My parents still didn't really know Elvis's intentions toward me. They only knew what I had told them. But they had also read in the newspapers that Elvis was dating every one of the female costars in his movies, so naturally they were suspicious.

One day on the phone I told Elvis, "If you want me to come back and go to school, you're going to have to talk to my father yourself."

"Put him on," Elvis replied. "I'm not MacArthur, but I can sure as hell try."

Drawing on all of his charm, Elvis assured my father that if I was permitted to move to Memphis, I wouldn't live with him at Graceland but with his daddy, Vernon, and his wife, Dee. Elvis promised to enroll me in a good Catholic school—he'd choose it himself—and make sure I graduated. He said I'd always be chaperoned and that he'd care for me in every way. Declaring his intentions honorable, he swore that he loved and needed and respected me. In fact, he couldn't live without me, he said, intimating that one day we'd marry.

This left my parents in a dilemma. If Elvis were as sincere as he sounded, there was a chance that our relationship might work out. But if it didn't work out, they ran the risk of my returning to them disillusioned and brokenhearted. If they refused to let me go, I might never forgive them and I would bitterly regret this unfulfilled love for the rest of my life. In that light, there was little they could do but say yes, and eventually they did.

In truth, I was as mystified as my parents were about why Elvis wanted me to come live with him. I think he was attracted by the fact that I had a normal, stable childhood, and that I was very responsible, having helped my parents raise my younger brothers and sister. I was more mature at sixteen than I was at fourteen, when he'd met me, not only because I'd gone through the normal growing period, but also because I'd experienced the pain of living without him for those two years.

Most of all, he knew he could depend on me. I wasn't interested in a career, in Hollywood, or in anything else that would draw my attention away from him. I also had all of the physical attributes that Elvis liked, the fundamentals he could use in turning me into his ideal woman. In short, I had everything that Elvis had been looking for in a woman: youth and innocence, total devotion, and no problems of my own. And I was hard to get.

I intended to do whatever I had to to hold him, because if he had ever sent me home, it would have meant not only that I'd been wrong in going to him, but that my parents had been wrong for having permitted it. I firmly resolved to make our relationship work, no matter what.

13

ELVIS SENT TWO first-class plane tickets. My father took
a leave of absence from his duties in Germany, and we
flew off to Los Angeles, where Elvis was filming *Fun in
Acapulco*.

We stayed at the Bel Air Sands Hotel, and Elvis was
the perfect host. He'd pick us up in either a white Rolls-
Royce or his famous gold Cadillac and take us on a
sightseeing tour along the ocean to Malibu or into Holly
wood.

My father was impressed with Elvis's hospitality, but
not enough to forget why he was there—to talk about
my education and my future at Graceland. Elvis didn't
want to jeopardize the deal they had already made, and
every time my father brought up my schooling, Elvis
would find a Hollywood landmark to point out.

"And over there, Captain," he said, changing the subject as we cruised down Hollywood Boulevard, "is Grauman's Chinese Theater. I'm sure you've heard of that. If you get out here, you can see all the stars of your era, their handprints and footprints. There's Betty Grable, you remember her, don't you? Marilyn Monroe, Kennedy's friend, and if you look hard enough, you might spot Trigger's hoofprint." As my father stepped out of the car, Elvis added, "I don't think MacArthur's are there yet, but I'm working on it." We all laughed at the incongruity of General MacArthur bending over the wet concrete next to Jane Russell.

After a few days, my father and I flew to Memphis and he and Vernon enrolled me in the school Elvis had chosen, Immaculate Conception, an all-girls high school, while Elvis himself remained in L.A. to finish the film.

Before I left, he assured me that he'd be home soon and that he'd see me in a few weeks.

Elvis and I planned to live together at Graceland eventually, but we'd told my parents that I would be staying with Vernon and Dee, so when I arrived in Memphis, I moved into their home. Vernon assured my father that I'd be in good hands and not to worry.

The concerned look on my father's face moved me. It was such a helpless look filled with doubts and fears about whether he was making the right decision. Only time would tell. He returned to Germany and I settled into my new routine.

In the beginning Vernon drove me to and from school, where word of my identity soon leaked out. As I walked down the hallway, heads would turn and whispers would start. Once, a note that was being passed in study hall ended up on the floor. I saw my name on it and picked it up.

"Her name's Priscilla," I read. "She's supposed to be Elvis Presley's new girlfriend. If we make friends with her, maybe she'll introduce us to him. Oh, God, wouldn't that be neat!"

I didn't know who the writer was, but I couldn't mistake the meaning. The friendly smiles concealed intentions to get to Elvis through me. Consequently, I was afraid to get close to anyone at school, and began to feel lonely and unhappy.

Living with Vernon and Dee was also difficult. I felt out of place in their home, and did not want to be an intrusion in their personal life. I began spending more time with Grandma at Graceland, often staying all night, and gradually, almost unnoticed, I began to move in my things. By the time Elvis suggested that I move into Graceland, I already had.

But living on "the hill," as we called it, was isolated. The only people there were Grandma and the maids, and during the day, the secretaries, Becky Yancy and Patsy Presley. Patsy was Elvis's double first cousin (her mother was Gladys's sister Cletis and her father was Vernon's brother Vester) and also served as Vernon's confidante. We were close, and after school I would go into the office to talk with her and Becky. But Vernon felt my visits kept the girls from working and finally he put a sign on the door specifying: NO ONE BELONGS IN THE OFFICE UNLESS THEY WORK THERE, OR HAVE AN APPOINTMENT. I knew that meant me too, so I curtailed my visits.

There were other restrictions. I was told that I couldn't have girlfriends over because strangers weren't allowed in the house. One day, I was severely criticized for sitting under the trees on the front lawn. I was playing with Honey, the poodle Elvis had given me for Christmas, when a friend of Dee's drove up and told me that I was making a public display of myself.

Even at school, I felt restricted because Vernon was still chauffeuring me there and back. Without my own car, I couldn't leave the school grounds to take a drive at lunch or when my classes were cut short. At last I asked Vernon if I could use Elvis's Lincoln Mark V and reluctantly, he agreed.

That evening I went for a drive. With the radio blaring and the windows wide open I sped down Highway 51 South, enjoying my newfound independence. I pulled up in front of Patsy Presley's house and said, "Hop in. Let's go for a drive."

Patsy introduced me to Leonard's Drive-In, where we would spend at least one night a week when we didn't go bowling or to a movie. But I went out less frequently when the two hundred dollars that my father had given me rapidly began slipping through my fingers. Elvis had assured my father not to worry about money, that if I needed any, his father would give it to me. So, with gas added to my expenses, I had no choice but to approach Vernon, as Elvis had instructed me.

Hesitantly I walked into his office. I was nervous about talking to Vernon, who had a sharp tongue and said exactly what he thought. Finally I said, "Mr. Presley, I was wondering if I could have some money. I'm spending a lot on gas, which doesn't leave much for anything else."

"How much do you think you need?" he asked, his eyes narrowing suspiciously.

"I . . . I don't know," I stammered.

He thought for a moment, then said, "Okay, I'll give you thirty-five dollars. How does that sound?"

Thirty-five dollars sounded fine at the moment, but it didn't go very far, not with movie tickets, gas, and clothes to buy. Two weeks later I asked him for money to go out with Patsy.

"Hot damn," he snapped. "Didn't I just give you thirty-five dollars?"

"That was two weeks ago, Mr. Presley. I can't stretch it any further than that."

He stared angrily at me and then his face softened.

"Well, I guess things can get pretty expensive," he said, counting out another thirty-five dollars. "Now you and Patsy be careful driving out there. You know there's a lot of accidents on that highway. Why don't you call me when you get to the theater?"

At the time his caution surprised me, but remembering what Elvis had said about Gladys, I knew that this was also typical of the rest of the Presleys. They always felt better if you called when you arrived at your destination and again before you left for home.

Elvis phoned later that evening. In the course of the conversation he asked, "How are you doing on cash, Baby?"

"Funny you should ask that," I said, mentioning his father's reaction when I asked for money.

Elvis started laughing. "That's my daddy. He's always been tight. Getting money from him is worse than going to the local bank, even if you've got good credit. That's why I have him taking care of my bills. Every penny's accounted for. I wouldn't trust anybody else. Too many thieves. Don't worry about it. I'll talk to him."

I ended up laughing too. Elvis's sense of humor was contagious. He laughed about things that often wouldn't make sense to anyone else, yet anyone around him would usually end up laughing too.

Unfortunately, Elvis forgot to speak to his father. Rather than ask for handouts, I resolved to earn my own money. I began modeling part-time at a boutique near Graceland. When I told Elvis about my job, he said, "You're gonna have to give it up."

"But I'm enjoying it," I said.

"It's either me or a career, Baby. Because when I call you, I need you to be there."

I quit the modeling job the next day, which left me with very little to do. I started spending even more time in Grandma's room. I liked being with her. She was always in her favorite chair, ready to share her loving stories about Elvis.

Most of them dealt with his early years and the family's struggle against poverty. Suffering and worry seemed to be the very fabric of the Presleys' lives. Any time Elvis failed to call home for two days in a row, they worried that something terrible had happened to him in California. Elvis's enormous success and wealth notwithstanding, they were convinced that some misfortune was going to snatch it all away from them. Sometimes all this talk of suffering depressed me.

My only relief was Patsy Presley, and I went to her every chance I got. But then Grandma complained that she was being neglected. She reminded me that Elvis's old girlfriends used to stay with her every single night he was gone. Torn, I couldn't wait for Elvis's return.

I anxiously waited for his call. It usually came in the early evening.

"Hi, Baby. How's my girl?" he asked, his voice bright and full of energy.

Happy to hear from him, I said, "I'm fine, Elvis." I tried to mention how lonely I was, but he cut in. "It won't be long, Baby. Just a few more weeks, and we'll be wrapping up."

"I'm glad. I'll be so happy to see you."

"Well, then, let me hear some enthusiasm." He began describing a silly incident that had taken place on the set that day, trying to make me laugh.

I wanted to say, "Elvis, talk to me, help me get

through these new experiences." But I realized that he didn't want to hear about my problems. He felt he had enough of his own. When he asked me how I was doing, I became very animated and said, "Just great, Elvis. Everything is wonderful."

But when we hung up, I still felt an emptiness. I began counting the days until he came home.

14

AFTER SEVERAL DELAYS Elvis finished *Fun in Acapulco* and headed back to Graceland. Still afraid of flying, he traveled with the entourage in his huge, custom-built bus, the same one we'd taken to Vegas the year before. At every stop he called Graceland with a progress report. "I'm in Flagstaff now," he said. "Only a few more days and I'll be home. How's my Little Girl doing?"

With each day's phone call I became increasingly excited. I awaited Elvis's arrival with open arms and a big smile.

Finally one evening he called and said he'd be pulling in around midnight. By ten o'clock, fans were already waiting at the gate. How they found out was a mystery. I was among a small group of his friends and relatives gathered in the living room. All of us peered impatiently out the large window facing the long circular driveway.

I had been hoping that our reunion would be intimate, romantic. But I could now see that it was not to be, and I wondered if Elvis would be upset that so many people were around.

By twelve-thirty, the fans at the gate started shrieking and the powerful glaring lights of the bus swept the driveway. Elvis was behind the wheel and smoothly brought the bus to a halt. He was the first one out and he came through the front door like a shot.

"Where's my Cilla?" he called out, looking around for me.

"Hello," I said. It seemed more like months than weeks since I'd last seen him.

"Hello?" he echoed in a mocking voice, coming up to me. "I've been gone all this time and all you can say is 'hello'?" Then he lifted me into the air, kissing and hugging me. "God, it's good to be home." He looked around and saw his grandma.

"Dodger, you waited up for me too, bless your heart." He hugged her and patted the back of her head. Then he greeted the rest of the household. Elvis could be extremely affectionate, and this particular night he had hugs for everyone.

With his arrival, Graceland sprang to life. The maids started cooking, and the boys were talking, greeting their wives and girlfriends, and soon they were bringing in the luggage and unpacking it.

After being alone so long, I found this sudden intensity and energy overpowering. I stood amid the commotion, watching Elvis go upstairs, as he called out to Alberta, "O Five, what's for dinner?"

I didn't know whether to follow him or wait. I didn't want to appear too excited, so I stayed downstairs until I heard, "Cilla, come up here." Then I couldn't get up those stairs fast enough.

We had a few quiet moments together in his room. He asked how I was doing, if I liked school, and if his daddy was taking care of me. I started to tell him everything I hadn't been able to on the phone, that I had missed him, that I had been lonely, that I really wanted to find a job. Then I stopped myself. This wasn't what Elvis wanted to hear.

After a few minutes of talking about Grandma, he kissed me and said, "Well, let's join the others and eat."

When we got downstairs the rooms that for weeks had been so quiet were now filled with guests laughing and cracking jokes.

Graceland was—as local DJ George Klein put it— ready to rock and roll.

We had a down-home meal of pork chops, cornbread, home fries, and crowder peas. While we were sitting around the table, local friends dropped by to visit and to catch up on all the gossip about Elvis's latest movie.

"Goddamn, she was a big woman," Elvis was saying about his costar. "Body like a man—no hips, and shoulders broader than mine. I was embarrassed to take my goddamn shirt off next to her."

"Yeah, but E," Alan Fortas kidded him, "she only had eyes for you."

"No way, Son, not with John Derek lurking all over

the place. I'd be goddamned if I'd start a conversation with her and see his possessive eyes glaring at me. You know he gave her a car, and on the steering wheel it said, 'Baby, you're indispensable.' Head over heels in love with her. Never saw anything like it."

I was surprised to hear how Elvis was talking about Ursula Andress, the alluring sex goddess of *Dr. No.*

"Wasn't she pretty?" I asked.

"Pretty?" he snickered. "Hell, she had a bone structure so sharp, it could cut you in half if you turned too fast."

Everyone howled, including me. Elvis's stories went on for hours. Again I felt out of touch with the conversation and wished I had some colorful stories of my own. I kept wondering when we were going to have some time alone. My world consisted solely of him. I sat quietly, happily observing him. Whenever he winked at me or gave my hand a little squeeze, I returned the gesture, thinking, *now?* Does he want me to leave, so he can follow me? But then he'd lean back in his chair and begin telling another story.

It was almost dawn before he yawned and said, "Well, we better get some sleep."

We all rose from the table. He looked over at me, smiled, and said, "Do I have to write a note for school saying you were sick today? Think they'd believe me?"

Everyone laughed—and I blushed.

He put his arm around my waist as we made our way up the staircase to his room. If I appeared cool it was because I was mindful of something he'd once told me: He detested aggressive women. In fact, I was ecstatic. I'm finally going to be alone with him, I thought. All the phone calls, the worrying, the anticipation, and the delays are now over.

I got ready for bed at least fifteen minutes before he came out of his bathroom. He counted out his usual number of sleeping pills and took them one at a time. "Why are you taking those now?" I asked. "You'll fall asleep." I had plans, and the last thing I wanted was for him to doze off.

"Don't worry. It'll take a while for them to take effect." He handed me a pill. "Here, just take one of these and you'll get a good night's sleep. It's okay since you're not going to school this morning." He cautioned, "I wouldn't advise it on school nights though."

I looked at the red monster, remembering my earlier experience with it. "It won't knock me out for ten days, will it?" I smiled at him as I swallowed the pill. It gave me a nice feeling. My body tingled. I was light-headed but more in control this time.

Snuggled in Elvis's arms, I was happy to be near him, his warm body against mine. Because of the sleeping pill, I could feel my inhibitions dissolving.

"How's my Little Girl been?" He was speaking very softly now. "I've missed her. Has she been good?"

"Yes, she's been good," I said. "But she's been waiting for you. It's been so lonely here. She couldn't wait to be in your arms, and she's been thinking about you so much."

"Shhh, don't say anything else. I know you've missed me. I want you to just be here with me now and don't think about anything else. Let's enjoy each other."

I was aware of the distant hum of the air conditioner, the music from the radio, the soft glow of the dim lights. Gently and tenderly he began to touch me.

He was passionate and again seemed to be making up for lost time. I felt sure the night would end with Elvis finally making love to me. I was drunk with ecstasy. I wanted him. I became bolder, reaching out to him, totally open and honest in my need.

Then, as before when we'd reach this point, he stopped and whispered, "Don't get carried away, Baby. Let me decide when it should happen. It's a very sacred thing to me. It always has been. You know that I want it to be something to look forward to. It keeps the desire there. Do you know what I mean?"

I sat up in anger. "What about Anita?" I yelled. "You mean you didn't make love to her the whole four years you went with her?"

"Just to a point. Then I stopped. It was difficult for her too, but that's just how I feel."

"That's how you feel. What about me? How long do you think this can go on? God, Elvis, that takes a lot of willpower. That's asking a lot of another person, one who's in love and has strong, healthy desires."

"Don't get me wrong. I'm not saying we can't do other things. It's just the actual encounter. I want to save it."

Fearful of not pleasing him—of destroying my image as his little girl—I resigned myself to the long wait.

Instead of consummating our love in the usual way, he began teaching me other means of pleasing him. We had a strong connection, much of it sexual. The two of us created some exciting and wild times.

It was the era of the Polaroid and the beginning of videotape. He was the director and I his star acting out fantasies. We dressed up and undressed, played and wrestled, told stories, acted out our fantasies, and invented scenes. Whether it was dressing up in my school uniform and playing at being a sweet, innocent schoolgirl, or a secretary coming home from work and relaxing in the privacy of her own bedroom, or a teacher seducing her student, we were always inventing new stories, and eventually, I learned what stimulated Elvis the most.

Almost every night I made quick trips to the local drugstore to buy considerable amounts of Polaroid film. Some of the cashiers knew me, and I wondered if they suspected what we were doing.

I put on dark glasses to "disguise" myself, but ended up looking even more conspicuous as I'd sweetly request twelve packs of Polaroid film while making excuses like, "Gee, the others must have been defective. I just can't seem to get them to come out right," or "You're not going to believe this, but someone stole my film."

Making it in and out of Graceland was no easy feat, either. I'd pass Mr. Stall at the gate at odd hours of the night, smiling and waving hello, returning shortly with the same smile and the same wave. I was sure he harbored some suspicious thoughts about what I was doing.

Elvis laughed when I told him. "It's all in your mind. He's no more thinking anything than a dog sleeping."

"Well, what if he starts spreading rumors, like I go out at night?"

"It might create some excitement around here. This town's dead. Memphis needs a little gossip!"

Elvis and I both loved creating these sexual fantasies and it seemed to bring us closer together. I had no previous sexual experience to compare with his inventive sexuality and I was ready to indulge him any way I could. Being in the fast lane, he was exposed to every pleasure available in life. Ordinary thrills sometimes were not enough, especially when he was under the influence of powerful drugs.

At first I was totally open to Elvis and many of his ideas. I lived for those moments we were alone. I was careful to say little that might jeopardize my bond with him. I fulfilled his needs, and his beliefs became mine. Under no circumstances were his ideas or playfulness perverted or in any way harmful.

15

A FEW DAYS after he came home, he led me to his long black limousine and we sped off to one of Memphis's most exclusive boutiques on Union Street for some after-hours shopping, just as we'd done in Las Vegas. While the boys milled around the shop and the store's sales staff tried to look nonchalant, Elvis got a big kick out of having me model dozens of stunning dresses and suits and coats that were so stylish I was doubtful I could wear them. I was still an insecure teenager.

"Elvis," I said, wearing a sexy gold lamé gown that clung to my every curve, "these clothes are too sophisticated for me."

"Sophisticated?" he said, regarding me admiringly. "What's sophisticated? You could go around wearing a feather and that would be sophisticated."

"Well, bring me a feather then."

We spent four hours at that shop and during that time, I had a personalized lesson in the Elvis Presley Fashion Course.

As I tried on dress after dress, Elvis delivered a running commentary on color. He liked me in red, blue, turquoise, emerald green, and black and white—the same colors he himself wore. He liked solids only, declaring that large prints took away from my looks. "Too distracting," he said. He hated browns and dark green, colors inextricably associated in his mind with the Army.

Exhausted and a little confused about my new look, I walked out of the shop dressed in a sleek black linen suit with four-inch high-heeled shoes to match. With Elvis sitting proudly beside me, the guys loaded the trunk of the limo with armfuls of packages, and I felt very special.

Back at Graceland he had me model all my new clothes again for Grandma, who patiently sat through a long two hours of changes. I was Elvis's doll, his own living doll, to fashion as he pleased.

It was the early sixties, when clothes and makeup veered to extremes. Women's eyeliner was heavier, their hair more teased, and their skirts shorter than ever before. All the rules I'd learned about dressing and applying makeup (less is more, the simpler the better) were being broken, and men seemed to love it. Elvis certainly did. If I went a little light with the mascara or black eyeliner, he'd send me back upstairs to apply it more heavily. Today I have to laugh when I look at the pictures taken of me then. I can hardly find my eyes under all that camouflage.

Elvis liked long hair. When I'd cut mine without asking his permission, he was shocked.

"How could you cut your goddamn hair? You know I like long hair. Men love long hair."

He wanted it long and jet black, dyed to match his because, as he said, "You have blue eyes, Cilla, like mine. Black hair will make your eyes stand out more." He made a lot of sense to me and soon my hair was dyed jet black, like his.

The more we were together the more I came to resemble him in every way. His tastes, his insecurities, his hang-ups—all became mine.

For instance, high collars were his trademark, not because he especially liked them, but because he felt his neck looked too long. He never felt comfortable unless he was in a customized high-collared shirt, though in a pinch he'd turn the collar up on a regular shirt as he had when he was in school.

When he told me that the collar I was wearing on a particular blouse was too small for my "long, skinny neck," I too began wearing high-collared shirts. Why not? My sole ambition was to please him, to be rewarded with his approval and affection. When he criticized me, I fell to pieces.

The Pygmalion nature of our relationship was a mixed blessing. The most fundamental thing at this stage in our life together was that Elvis was my mentor, someone who studied my every gesture, listened critically to my every utterance, and was generous, to a fault, with advice.

When I did something that wasn't to his liking, I was corrected. It is extremely difficult to relax under such scrutiny. Little escaped him. Little except the most salient fact of all—that I was a volcano about to erupt.

There were evenings when he'd send me back upstairs to change clothes because my choice was "dull," "unflattering," or "not dressy enough" for him. Even the way I walked came under review; he told me to move more slowly, and for a short while, he had me walking around the house with a book on my head.

I appreciated his interest, but I hated having to hear him remind me of my shortcomings so many times, and each time having to promise him that he'd never have to tell me again.

Would I ever be able to live up to his vision of how his ideal woman should behave and appear? She had to be sensitive, loving, and extremely understanding, meeting unusual demands any average woman might reject. This included being left behind when he made spur-of-the-moment, questionable "business" trips.

She had to be pretty and she had to possess an offbeat sense of humor to survive all the joking at Graceland. Often I'd walk into Sunday afternoon football gatherings and hear inside jokes about the cute all-American cheerleaders. Eventually I found myself thinking like one of the guys. "Nice tits and ass," I'd say to myself. "A little heavy in the thighs, but the face makes up for it."

Elvis had a strong aversion to wearing jeans. As a poor boy, he had no choice but to wear them and he never wanted to lay eyes on another pair. That applied to everyone in the group.

His firm ideas on my wardrobe didn't make it easy for me to go out and buy clothes for myself. One day I came home proud of a dress I'd just bought and couldn't wait to put on. I knew he didn't like prints, but this was a black-and-white flowered silk that I thought very special.

The first words out of his mouth when he saw me were: "That dress doesn't suit you. Does nothing for you. Takes away from your face, your eyes. All you see's the dress."

As he tore me apart I started to cry. "Are you quite finished?" I inquired. I didn't give him a chance to answer, bolting for my bathroom and slamming the door.

A few minutes later I heard his voice from the other side of the door: "You gotta keep away from those large prints. You're a small girl, Sattnin."

I opened the bathroom door and snapped, "Okay, I'll return the fuckin' dress."

Elvis fell to the floor laughing; eventually I joined in, unable to stop myself. Once again I'd compromised my own taste.

He ignored no aspect of my appearance, including my teeth. He took me to his dentist, told him to clean my teeth and give me a thorough examination. He was to look for probable cavities only and should I need any fillings, they were to be made of white porcelain. To him a mouth loaded with gold or silver was an eyesore.

He was equally fanatical about posture. If I slumped, he'd straighten my back. When I'd look up at him and wrinkle my forehead, he'd smooth it out—or tap it—telling me not to get in that habit. I didn't like him rapping me, so I learned that one fast.

When we came home from the movies one night, I was getting ready for bed and he was in his office playing the piano. I came in to listen, propping my foot on the bench where he was sitting. He looked down at a small chip in my nail polish and I immediately withdrew my foot from the bench and started making up excuses about why it wasn't fixed. "I'm going to have my pedicure to-morrow," I promised.

"Good," he said, "cause that doesn't look like my Little Girl's pretty sooties. You should always keep them looking nice."

I was leading a double life—a schoolgirl by day, a femme fatale by night. Our evening appearance downstairs usually resembled a grand entrance. Even when our only intention was to have dinner, we always dressed for the occasion. Elvis might wear a three-piece suit with a brocade vest and a Stetson hat. Under his coat he always carried a gun. He'd given me a small pearl-handled derringer and I carried it in my bra or tucked it into a holster around my waist. We were a modern-day Bonnie and Clyde.

Elvis loved films, and we went to the Memphian almost every night. He was still renting the whole house after regular hours since he couldn't attend a movie without being mobbed. One of the guys always lined up several films in case Elvis didn't like one of them or decided to see as many as three or four in a row. We usually arrived around midnight, our limousine pulling around to the back of the Memphian. From there we'd proceed into the side door like a royal couple leading their court.

Already seated in the theater were the usual crowd of thirty to fifty local friends and fans. Elvis always sat in the same seat—with Joe Esposito to his right, me to his left.

Before calling *"Roll 'em!"* he looked around the theater to make sure everyone was seated. He was an acutely aware person and could immediately spot any unwanted or unfamiliar faces. If any new faces were sitting too close to him, Elvis suggested they move elsewhere. He was more lenient with the girls. He might not demand they move but he certainly wanted to know who they were, and should they object to being asked for this information or smart off in any way, he would not hesitate to have one of the boys escort them out, telling them never to come back.

There were times Elvis rented the entire Memphis Fairgrounds after closing and we all spent hours on our favorite rides. We tried such daredevil feats on the roller-coaster as seeing who could stand the longest with both arms outstretched as it whipped and twisted around the track again and again.

Elvis loved the bumper cars and would team up with the entourage against some locals. They'd spend the night seemingly trying to kill each other, laughing and bruising themselves like tough little boys while we girls watched and cheered them on. After several hours my own enthusiasm waned.

16

ELVIS PRESLEY CREATED his own world; only in his own environment did he feel secure, comfortable, and protected. A genuine camaraderie was created at Graceland. We lived as one big family, eating, talking, arguing, joking, playing, and traveling together.

Although I became friends with the guys in Elvis's retinue, he never let me, or anyone else, forget that I was his girl. I was never to get too close or become too familiar with any of the regulars.

One evening, after we came home from a movie, we said good night to everyone and went upstairs. Returning to the kitchen a few minutes later to get something to eat, I found Jerry Schilling, who'd just started working for Elvis, making himself a snack. We started talking. A few minutes later, Elvis appeared.

"What the hell are you two doing down here?" he shouted at us.

Intimidated, Jerry said, "Well, Elvis, we were just talking. I was asking her how she felt, because she didn't feel well this afternoon."

"I came down to get something to eat," I explained.

"Cilla, you don't need to be roaming around here late at night," he said, angrily ordering me upstairs.

Behind me, I could hear him lashing out at Jerry. "If you want to keep this job, son, you mind your own business. If there's anyone who's going to ask her how she feels, it'll be me. You better mind your own goddamn business."

I liked Jerry. He was warm, sincere, and very personable; just a couple of years older than I, he was one of the few people whom I could relate to. But from that time on, it was a dodging match every time we'd run into each other. Now Jerry and I laugh about the "good ol' days" when we reminisce.

Most of the boys who worked for Elvis had been around from the beginning and they knew all about him—his sense of humor, his sensitivity, and his temper. He stripped himself bare in front of them, and they accepted him for what he was.

Yet working for Elvis was a twenty-four-hour-a-day job, and the boys were at his beck and call constantly. They played when he played and slept when he slept. It took a certain kind of personality to put up with his demands, whether they made sense or not.

"Come on, Cilla, let's go to Tupelo, Mississippi. I'll show you where I was born," he said one afternoon when we'd only been up for a few hours. He called downstairs and told Alan to alert everyone that he wanted to leave within the hour.

Alan said, "Okay, Boss. I think Richard and Gene are still sleeping. I'll give 'em a call and tell 'em to come right over."

"Their lazy asses are still sleeping?" Elvis asked. "I've been up for two goddamn hours. They should have been over here by now. Alan, from now on, when I call down for my breakfast, call the boys and tell them I'm up and to be ready for anything, and that may include me not even coming downstairs. I just want them here."

Demanding? Yes, but Elvis could be just as generous. By today's standards the boys' salaries were not high— the average paycheck was $250 a week—but if the boys ever felt the pinch by the end of the month, they would go to Elvis. They'd ask him if he could help them out with a down payment on a house or the first and last months' payments on an apartment. Elvis *always* came through for them, lending them the one thousand or five thousand or ten thousand dollars they asked for. He was rarely if ever paid back.

There also was no limit to the expensive gifts he gave them—television consoles for Christmas, bonus checks, Cadillac convertibles, Mercedes-Benzes. If he heard someone was sad or depressed, he loved to surprise them with a gift, usually a brand-new car. When he gave to one, he would usually end up giving to all.

Vernon didn't have much respect for the guys. He said Elvis just gave and gave and gave, and they took and took and took. He'd say, "Son, we have to save." Elvis would answer, "It's only money, Daddy. I just have to go out and make more."

Vernon resented the regulars acting as if Graceland was their personal club. They'd go into the kitchen at any hour and order anything they wanted. Naturally, everyone ordered something different. The cooks worked night and day keeping them happy. Vernon felt, "To hell with the boys. Their main concern should be Elvis."

What was really outrageous was that the regulars were ordering sirloin steaks or prime ribs while Elvis usually ate hamburgers or peanut butter and banana sandwiches.

I wasn't too popular around Graceland when I started reorganizing the kitchen. I set down a policy of having one menu per meal, and anyone who didn't like what was on it could go to a local restaurant. This new edict resulted in much grumbling from the guys, but the cooks were relieved, and Vernon sanctioned my decision, announcing, "It's about time someone organized the meals. It was beginning to look like we were feeding half of Memphis."

Elvis was the boss, the provider, and the power. Both the boys and I had to protect him from people who annoyed or irritated him and were no longer in his favor. Before coming down for the evening, he'd have me call downstairs to check who was there. I'd run down the guests, aware that certain names would strike him wrong.

"Shit," he'd say, his mood destroyed. "What's he want? Bring me some more bad news?" He'd stay up in his room rather than spend an evening with someone he didn't like. There was one particular regular who had incurred his disfavor, and Elvis told everyone he didn't want him around. "Don't let him through those god-damn gates!" Elvis ordered. "All I have to do is look at his face and I get depressed." Elvis barred him from Graceland for a number of years, saying, "If he changes his morbid attitude, maybe I'll change my mind." His perceptions were correct, as these "friends" eventually betrayed him.

Elvis and Vernon kept some of their relatives at a distance because, as Elvis explained to me, they'd shunned him when he was growing up, ridiculing him as a sissy, a mama's boy. Gladys stood up for Elvis and told his tormentors to go their own way. Angrily, she had said, "Don't bother us with these accusations."

Then fame and fortune hit, and suddenly all the kinfolk came around, begging for jobs or crying that they needed help. Sometimes Elvis got upset, charging, "The only time they visit is with their hand out. It'd be nice if they'd come around just to see how I was doing. But hell no, it's always, 'Ah, Elvis, I could use a little extra cash. Could you help me out?' Hell, I'll bet when I'm dead and gone, they'll still be taking advantage." But Elvis ended up slipping each of them a hundred dollars or more every time they came around. If it had been up to

Vernon, he would have gotten rid of every one of them. But Elvis kept saying, "No, Daddy, they don't have any place to go. They couldn't work anywhere. Keep them here."

From the beginning of his success, Elvis put many family members on salary, and all had titles. Vernon was his business manager; Patsy, his personal secretary; uncles Vester Presley and Johnny and Travis Smith, and cousin Harold Lloyd, gate guards; cousins Billy, Bobby, and Gene, personal aides; and then there was Tracy Smith, who seemed to go from brother to brother for support. Elvis took care of everyone.

I remember one night at Graceland when Elvis came back to the kitchen and saw Tracy pacing the floor. "Hey, Tracy," he said, "How ya doing, man?" Tracy, his hands in his pockets, could hardly look Elvis in the eye. "I don't know, Elvis," he sighed. "What do ya mean, you don't know? Everyone knows how they're doin', man."

Tracy, shifting back and forth, mumbled, "I got my nerves in the dirt, Elvis." Elvis staggered back, laughing. "Nerves in the dirt! Hell, I never heard it expressed like that before. You need some money, Tracy?"

Again, Tracy just shifted back and forth, as Elvis called Joe over and told him to give Tracy a bill. A big smile covered Tracy's lined face as he happily took his hundred dollars and walked out the door.

Elvis knew that having his nerves in the dirt was Tracy's way of saying he was down and out—and worried sick about it. He never forgot that phrase. "Poor ol'

Tracy," he'd say. "I'll never forget the look on his face that night, poor ol' guy."

That was Elvis—always caring, always sensitive to everyone's needs, even while presenting a macho image to his fans and friends.

17

ANYTHING I COULD think of doing for him, I did. I made sure Graceland was always warm and inviting, with the lights turned low, as he preferred them, the temperature in his bedroom set to his exact desire (freezing), and the kitchen filled with the aroma of his favorite meals.

Every night before dinner was served, I came downstairs first, checked with the maids to see that his food was just the way he liked it—his mashed potatoes creamily whipped, plenty of cornbread, and his meat burnt to perfection. I always had candles on the dining room table to create a romantic atmosphere despite the fact that we always ate with several of the regulars.

I loved babying Elvis. He had a little-boy quality that could bring out the mother instinct in any woman, a beguiling way of seeming utterly dependent. It was this aspect of his charm that made me want to hold him, shower him with affection, protect him, fight for him, and yes, even die for him. I went to extremes in taking care of him, from cutting his steak at dinner to making sure his water glass was always filled. I enjoyed pampering and spoiling him and found myself jealous of others vying for his attention and approval.

But I didn't always receive his approval. If something went wrong with his dinner, Elvis blew up. "Why isn't this steak done? Why didn't you make sure the maids cooked it right? If you'd have done your job, it wouldn't have turned out like this." Obviously something else was wrong, and I didn't recognize it at the time. Because of the continuous pressures and problems in Elvis's life, all magnified by taking prescribed drugs, little things would set him off. I took responsibility for everything in his life and always took it all too personally.

I wanted to be with Elvis as much as I could, but while going to the movies or the fairgrounds every night might have been a wonderful way for him to relax, it posed an enormous problem for me. Often I wouldn't get home until 5 or 6 A.M., and I'd have to be at school two hours later. Sometimes I never went to sleep. When I did, I could barely make it out of bed. I would lie there trying to drum up the strength to face the day, Elvis making it even harder by suggesting that I sleep in and cut classes. It would have been so easy to go along with his suggestion, but hanging over me was the agreement I'd made with my parents. They trusted me and even though I was letting them down, I still had to keep up the facade.

Day after day I drove to school, attended classes till noon, then returned to Graceland to slip back into bed and cuddle next to Elvis, who was still sound asleep. When he awoke at 3 or 4 P.M., I might never have left his side for all he knew. I was there to give him his usual order of orange juice, a Spanish omelet, home-fried potatoes, a mere two pounds of bacon, and—first and foremost—his black coffee.

Everyone who knew Elvis was aware that it took him at least two to three hours to wake up fully. Asking him to make a decision, even a simple one such as what movie he wanted to see that night, was ill-advised. He was just too groggy and irritable from the sleeping pills, which were causing him to sleep as many as fourteen hours a day. It seemed only natural for him to take some Dexedrine to wake up.

I was always concerned about his intake of sleeping pills. His horror of insomnia, compounded with a family history of compulsive worrying, caused him to down three or four Placidyls, Seconals, Quaaludes, or Tuinals almost every night—and often it was a combination of all four. When I expressed my concern, he just picked up the medical dictionary, always near at hand on his night table.

"In here is the explanation for every type of pill on the market, their ingredients, side effects, cures, everything about them," he assured me. "There isn't anything I can't find out."

It was true. He was always reading up on pills, always checking to see what was on the market, and which ones had received FDA approval. He referred to them by their medical names and knew all their ingredients. Like everyone else around him, I was impressed with his knowledge and certain that he was an expert. One would think he had a degree in pharmacology. He always assured me that he didn't *need* pills, that he could never become dependent on them. This difference in opinion resulted in many serious confrontations; I always compromised my integrity and ended up taking his viewpoint.

I began taking sleeping pills and diet pills too. Two Placidyls for him and one for me. A Dexedrine for him and one for me. Eventually Elvis's consumption of pills seemed as normal to me as watching him eat a pound of bacon with his Spanish omelet. I routinely took "helpers" in order to get to sleep after wild rides at the fairgrounds or early-morning jam sessions. And I routinely took more "helpers" when I woke up in order to maintain the fast pace and, more importantly, to study for my final exams.

During the last month before finals, I started popping more dexies than before. They seemed to give me the energy I needed to get through classes and homework. Every free moment was devoted to cramming a whole semester's work into a few weeks. But my concentration was scattered; the strain of life at Graceland had finally caught up with me.

I had already been warned by Sister Adrian that in order for me to graduate, I had to pass all my subjects. During a talk in her office, I wanted desperately to confide in her and explained how hard it was to maintain my grade level with the late hours I kept. But how could I tell that to a nun?

I had no real goals after graduation, but I did sometimes dream of becoming a dancer or possibly enrolling in an art academy. Now I realize that I was deeply influenced by Elvis's casual attitude toward continued schooling. He figured I didn't need it and I agreed. Just being with him most of the time would provide an education—not to mention experience—that no school could give me. He wanted me to be his totally, free to go to him in an instant if he needed me.

That sounded great to me. I'd never planned on a future without Elvis. Therefore, while my classmates were deciding which colleges to apply to, I was deciding which gun to wear with what sequined dress. I was tempted to say to Sister Adrian, "Oh, by the way, Sister, does gunmetal gray go with royal blue sequins?" With that attitude it was no surprise that I was still woefully unprepared for my most hated subject, algebra, the week before finals.

On the day of the test, I sat in the crowded classroom, hyper from downing a dexy, trying to work out the problems. Despite my effort, I knew there was no way I was going to pass. I started to panic. I *had* to graduate. I had an obligation to Elvis and to my parents, who I knew would yank me out of Graceland the minute I failed this test. I glanced at the girl next to me—*and* at her completed test paper. It's my last resort, I thought. I'm going for it. I was not willing to face the consequences of being sent home for failing this test.

Her name was Janet and she was a straight-A student. I tapped her on the shoulder and flashed my brightest smile, whispering, "Are you an Elvis fan?" Taken aback by my question, Janet nodded yes. "How would you like to come to one of his parties?" I asked.

"Are you kidding?" she replied. "I'd love to."

"Well, I know a way that it can be arranged."

I eyed her test paper and explained. Janet instantly grasped my dilemma and, without a word, slid her paper to the edge of her desk. Now I had a full view of her answers. I spent the rest of the hour furiously copying them down and I not only passed, but I got an A on that test.

18

I HADN'T EXPECTED Elvis to make much of my graduation. His attitude was, "A diploma's not that important; life's experiences are." But to my surprise, he really looked forward to it and arranged to have a big party for our friends after the ceremony. There he presented a beautiful red Corvair, my first car.

On the big night he was like a proud parent. Nervous about what he should wear to the ceremony, he finally settled on a dark blue suit, and I put on my navy blue gown. I couldn't possibly keep the cap on over that mass of teased hair.

Elvis had a limo waiting for us out front. But there was one problem: I did not want him to come to the actual ceremony. It would attract a lot of attention, and all eyes would be focused on him instead of the graduating seniors.

Finally I worked up enough courage to ask him to wait outside, and explained why. Smiling his funny little grin, the one that came to his lips when he was hurt or upset, he agreed without hesitation. "I hadn't thought about that," he said. "I won't come in. I'll just be outside in the car waiting for you. That way I'll kinda be there."

And that was what he did. I accepted my diploma with mixed emotions. I would have loved for him to have been watching, but only I knew what a physical, emotional, and mental strain it had been to get that piece of paper. To me, it represented freedom, freedom to stay out until dawn if I wanted and sleep all day if I wanted. It represented freedom from my school uniform and from the teasing the entourage subjected me to every time they caught me in it trying to sneak past them at Graceland. I was a big girl playing in the big leagues.

As soon as I could get away, I ran outside. In front of the church, Elvis and the boys were standing by the long black limo, looking like the Chicago Mafia in their dark glasses and suits, each concealing a .38. Around them a group of nuns were clamoring for Elvis's autograph.

When he looked up and saw me, he began applauding along with the boys. Hugging me, he told me how proud he was. He had me unroll the diploma so he could see it. I had finally graduated.

Now I could spend every minute with Elvis. There were times when we'd shut outselves off from the rest of the world for days. Elvis would leave word that he wanted "no calls unless it's my daddy or an emergency call from Colonel." It was my time, and no one could interfere. He was all mine.

When we got hungry, I phoned down to the kitchen and ordered our food, which was brought up and placed outside our bedroom door. After we finished, we stacked our empty trays neatly back in the same place.

We saw no one, nor even the light of day. The windows were insulated with tin foil and heavy blackout drapes to prevent any hint of sunlight from entering. Time was ours, to do with as we pleased, for as long as we pleased. Elvis had a few months free between film commitments, and there was no pressure to return to Hollywood.

We always seemed to be more in love when we were alone. I loved those times, when he was just Elvis, not trying to live up to an image or a myth. We were two people discovering each other.

Only in the privacy of our own quarters did Elvis show me a side of himself which had rarely, if ever, been seen by others. With no Colonel, no scripts, no films or music, nor any other people's problems, Elvis could become a little boy again, escaping from the responsibilities of family, friends, fans, the press, and the world. Here with me, he could be vulnerable and childlike, a playful boy who stayed in his pajamas for days at a time.

One day he was the dominant one and would treat me like a child, often scolding me for an incidental action.

On other days I was the stronger one, looking after him like a doting mother, making sure that he ate everything on his plate, took all of his vitamins, and didn't miss any of his favorite TV shows like *Laugh-In*, *The Untouchables*, *The Wild, Wild West*, *The Tonight Show*, and *Road Runner*.

We listened to early Sunday morning gospel singing—our favorites were the Stamps, the Happy Goodman Family, and Jake Hess—and we watched the old movie classics that Elvis loved: *Wuthering Heights*, *It's a Wonderful Life*, and *Miracle on 34th Street*.

We cried ourselves to sleep over *The Way of All Flesh*, which concerns a banker who plans to carry a large sum of money out of state, only to discover upon awakening the following morning that he has been robbed. Stripped of everything, he takes to the streets, surviving among the derelicts, an outcast. Years later, one Christmas night, he wanders into his hometown and peers through the window to see his wife and children, now grown, opening their presents. Sensing his presence but never recognizing him, his wife takes pity on the lonely old man and invites him in to share the evening with her family. He declines, heading down the snowy street alone. Elvis identified so thoroughly with the story that he toyed with the idea of a remake. He intended to cast Vernon in the lead role.

There were other favorites we'd watch over and over—*Mr. Skeffington* with Bette Davis and Claude Rains, *Les Miserables* with Fredric March, Charles Laughton, and Rochelle Hudson, and *Letter from an Unknown Woman* with Joan Fontaine.

When we weren't watching movies, we played silly games like hide-and-seek, or we'd have pillow fights that often ended in heated discussions of who hit whom the hardest. Our arguments were usually playful, but I noticed that they could become serious, especially after we'd each taken a couple of diet pills.

One evening we had both taken uppers and were wrestling with each other. I threw a pillow at him. He ducked it, and then, laughing, threw it back. I hurled another one at him, and then another, and without giving him a chance to recover, I threw another one. The last one hit him in the face. His eyes flashed with anger.

"Goddamn it!" he snapped. "Not so rough. I don't want to play with a goddamn man." He grabbed my arm, throwing me on the bed, and while demonstrating how hard I had thrown the pillows, he accidentally hit me in the eye. I flung my head to the side and jumped up, accusing him of hitting me on purpose.

"You can't play without winning," I yelled, "even with me. You started throwing harder and harder. What did you expect me to do?"

I stomped off to my dressing room and slammed the door as I heard him yelling, "You're not a goddamn man."

That night, we went to the movies. My arm was bruised where he'd grabbed me, and my eye was swollen black and blue. To make matters worse—and to make sure he felt bad—I wore a patch over the bruised eye. Everyone teased me, and Elvis joked, "Couldn't help it. She tried to get rough with me. I had to show her who's boss."

That night I got named "Toughie."

Despite his teasing, Elvis felt terrible about the incident. He had immediately apologized to me and kept apologizing for days.

"Baby, I'm really sorry," he said. "You know I'd never hurt you in any way, that I'd never lay a hand on you, don't you? That was a real accident."

Yet the incident frightened me.

From then on, I began taking fewer pills and eventually stopped. I tried to persuade him to do the same. I started to question the quantities even though I knew he had various ailments causing pain which necessitated taking prescribed medication. I did everything I could for Elvis and we shared many wonderful happy times together. However, his harsh objection to stopping made me realize that there could be a problem. I assumed he knew best for himself.

19

COLONEL PARKER'S theory was: "If you want to see Elvis Presley, you buy a ticket." Once you started passing out freebies, it meant a lot of lost income. He stuck to that policy to the day Elvis died.

Elvis agreed with the Colonel, feeling that Colonel knew best, saying, "Colonel doesn't mind taking the blame."

When life got boring you could count on Elvis to concoct some new escapade. He was extraordinarily inventive. One particularly dreary day he decided out of the blue that he didn't like the looks of an old house located on the grounds in back of the mansion. His uncle Travis had once occupied the place, which was now used for storage. Elvis took a long look at it, called his father, and told him to get a bulldozer over there right away and get rid of it.

I could imagine what was going through Vernon's mind: Good God, what's he up to now? He knew if Elvis was at home and bored between films, anything could happen.

When the bulldozer appeared, Elvis insisted that he was going to do the honors, convincing his father—and the local fire and demolition departments—that he could handle the job himself.

Wearing his football helmet and his big furry Eskimo coat, Elvis proceeded, as his entourage cheered him on, to bring down the house and set it afire. This brought the fire trucks screaming through the gates. "You're a little late, fellows," Elvis said, a happy, mischievous smile on his face.

Another time, he ordered his go-carts to be brought out and readied to ride. He held the record, of course, for the fastest time around the large circular drive.

Trying to prove that I was just as good as the guys, I tried to equal his time. Terrified, I would speed along as Elvis clocked me on his stopwatch, giving me an approving grin when I reached the fifteen-mile-per-hour mark.

He turned Graceland into a private playground for us all. He'd have gun-shooting contests and also "screaming thrill rides" when he'd pack several people into his custom-built golf cart and race around the grounds at top speed.

Graceland's backyard had more holes in it than the moon has craters—all from Roman-candle fights. On the

Fourth of July Elvis always spent a fortune on fireworks, which arrived by the boxload. The boys would team up sides, aim candles directly at one another, and fire.

Although there were casualties—burned fingers and singed hair—no one seemed to care. Elvis himself was as carefree as a young kid, hiding and then sneaking around the opposition with surprise attacks. Elvis knew how to play hard and have fun. I miss those times.

Unfortunately, the time came for him to go back to Hollywood. He was due to begin his new film, *Viva Las Vegas*. His bus was parked in front of the white stone lions flanking the front steps of Graceland, loaded and ready to go.

I hated to see him leave. Arm in arm, we walked out the door.

Suddenly I pulled him back and tried to tell him what I was feeling, but there were distractions all around— people saying goodbye, music blaring from inside the bus, Alan yelling to George Klein to keep the sound rockin' and rollin'.

I thought, If only it were quieter, if only Elvis would take me aside so we could have some privacy.

But his attention was on all the activity and he was caught up in the excitement of going back to work.

"What is it, Baby?" he asked.

"I just wish you didn't have to leave so soon," I said,

still unable to tell him what was really on my mind. "Just when we were starting to get used to each other, you have to go. I wish there were more time."

"I know, Little One. Just give me a couple of weeks to get into the film and maybe you can come out for a while. Be a good girl, and I'll call you tomorrow."

He gave me a quick kiss on the lips and boarded the bus, the doors slamming shut behind him. Then I heard the familiar shout, "All right. Let's roll it!"

With a roar, the bus cruised down the hill and through the Music Gates where, as always, his fans were loyally waving goodbye and urging him to "hurry home!"

I watched until I could no longer see the red taillights fading out on Highway 51.

Cursing myself, I wondered why I couldn't tell him what I feared. I'd been upset ever since I'd learned that his new leading lady was going to be Ann-Margret, the fastest-rising starlet in Hollywood. Ann-Margret had made only a few movies, including *Bye-Bye Birdie*, but she'd been dubbed "the female Elvis Presley." Elvis was curious about her, pointing out that "imitation is the sincerest form of flattery."

I realized that even had I told him my fears, he could have said nothing to put my mind at ease, because one evening he had made the mistake of telling me about the romances he'd had with many of his costars. Trying to listen calmly to these stories, I justified his behavior by reminding myself that I'd been living in Germany during those years and that we'd had no real ties then.

Now I was in his territory, living in his house with his friends, his family, and mementos of the past. It didn't occur to me then, but I was living the way he wished—out of Hollywood society, the girl back home. I adapted. I wasn't with him, but in a sense I was. And I assumed that he would be as faithful to me as I was to him.

Why, then, was I so sure that once Elvis was far away from me—and very near to Ann-Margret—an affair would develop?

20

❧

EACH TIME I would get ready to join Elvis in Los Angeles he would delay my visit.

"Baby, now's not the time to come out. There's a problem on the set."

"What kind of problem?"

"It's just that all hell's broke loose. I've got some crazed director madly in love with Ann. The way he's directing it, you'd think it was her movie. He's favoring her in all the goddamn close-up shots." He paused, his anger rising. "Not only that, they want her to sing some of the songs with me. Colonel 'bout blew a fuse. Told 'em they'd have to pay me extra to sing with her."

As I listened to Elvis rant and rave, I tried to sympathize with him and his situation, but emotionally I was far more concerned about his leading lady than his director.

"Well, how are you and Ann-Margret getting along?" I asked.

"Oh, she's okay, I guess." He casually dismissed her with the line, "a typical Hollywood starlet."

My concern was temporarily allayed. I knew that his attitude toward actresses was unfavorable. "They're into their careers and their man comes second," he'd say. "I don't want to be second to anything or anyone. That's why you don't have to worry about my falling in love with my so-called leading ladies."

I wanted to believe him, but I couldn't help noticing the national gossip magazines and the headlines about the torrid affair on the set of *Viva Las Vegas*. The problem was that the affair was not between Ann-Margaret and the director. It was between Ann-Margaret and Elvis.

We were talking on the phone one night and I asked, "Is there anything to it?"

"Hell, no," he said, immediately becoming defensive. "You know how these reporters are. They blow everything out of proportion. She comes around here mostly on weekends with her motorcycle. She hangs out and jokes with the guys. That's it."

But that was enough for me: She was there and I wasn't.

Infuriated, I declared, "I want to come out now."

"No, not now! We're wrapping up the film and I'll be home in a week or two. You keep your little ass there and keep the home fires burning."

"The flame's burning on low. Someone had better come home and start the fire."

Elvis laughed. "You're beginning to sound like me," he bragged. "I'd better watch it. There can't be two of us walking around. I'll be home soon, Baby. Get everything ready." By the end of our phone call, I was eagerly making plans for his return.

I took out my calendar, counted the days until his homecoming, and then crossed them off one at a time. Threatened with doubts and fears, I did everything I could to please him, from educating myself about the gospel music he loved to taking good care of Graceland.

My eagerness to please Elvis was so overwhelming that it almost angered him. He always had an excuse why his other relationships hadn't worked out. "They were either too hometown and couldn't fit in with my Hollywood life-style," he said, "or they were actresses too into their careers." But how could he get out of a commitment to such a willing partner as me?

I often felt sorry for myself, and angry at Elvis for putting me in a situation in which I was forced to be alone for literally weeks at a time.

Bored, I resorted to exploring the attic at Graceland. I'd asked Grandma once what was up there, and she'd answered, "Oh, nothin', Hon, jus' some old junk. God, I haven't been up there in ages. No tellin' what's up there—or who."

There was no question that something was stirring around in the attic. Many nights strange noises were heard above the kitchen. Grandma said she'd heard the noises herself, lying awake, praying for daylight before even closing her eyes for sleep.

She imagined that it might be Gladys's spirit up there, watching over Elvis.

"Do you believe in spirits, Grandma?" I asked.

"Ah, yes, Hon. Sometimes I wander through this house and I can just feel 'em all around. Ask Hattie, she knows. She's felt 'em too."

Hattie was a large black woman, our faithful and devoted companion. She stayed with Grandma and me at night while Elvis was away, guarding us with her life— and a small gun that she tucked securely under the bed each night.

One evening, after Hattie turned out the lights, I asked her, "Hattie, do you think there's spirits there, like Grandma does?"

"Well, Miss Priscilla, all I can tell you is that I hear strange voices I ain't never heard before in any house I've ever been in, and sometimes it gits awful quiet here, a kind of stillness that I ain't never felt neither. But don't you lay there and worry, child. If there are any spirits, they'll do you no harm."

"Amen," Grandma said.

The next day, I decided to venture up to the attic, to see for myself what was there. As I walked up the stairs, I rubbed my hand up and down the gold-painted banister, noting the chipped paint. I called out, "Don't you think this should be repainted, Dodger?"

Grandma, standing at the bottom of the stairs, lifted her dark shades to get a closer look. "Yes, Hon, we'd better tell Vernon. That does look bad."

"Maybe we should do it before Elvis gets home and surprise him. I'll ask Mr. Presley in the morning."

At the top of the stairs I entered the attic and discovered Elvis's world.

Several trunks were filled with his military gear. There were old television sets and furniture that had been in his bedroom years before. I ran my hand over a couch, wondering who'd sat there with him. Jealous, I walked away.

I found two closets side by side and opened one. It was filled with clothes from Elvis's early days—black leather jackets, motorcycle hats, and a pink shirt I'd seen in pictures. I loved the way he looked in that shirt and wished he'd wear it again.

With growing curiosity, I sorted through everything. I felt closer to Elvis just by touching his things, and all I could think of was what girl he'd been with at the time—Dixie, Judy, Anita, Bonnie? I was so possessive, I had to know.

Then I came across some letters hidden under an old sweater, letters from Anita, all addressed to him in Germany. I put them in dated order, from his arrival in Germany to his departure, and sat there for hours poring over every one.

Anita had written at least two letters a week, all saying basically the same thing: she loved him, missed him, and was counting the days until his return—just as I had done. She had been in the process of acquiring him as a lover just as I'd been losing him. Clearly Elvis had been telling her that she was the only one in his life. Confused and hurt, I realized that he had been writing to his "Little Bit," as he called her, that he couldn't wait to come home and see her, at the same time that he had been holding me tightly, telling me he couldn't bear to leave his "Little Girl."

I felt betrayed, as I'm sure she felt when she read and heard about me.

Returning the next day to investigate the adjoining closet, I came upon Gladys's belongings—her clothes, her old photos and papers. It was strange to see all her dresses, hanging neatly. I knew Elvis had had them put there. He couldn't have faced throwing away any of her personal belongings.

I tried on one of her dresses and could tell that she liked soft materials on her skin, just as I did. By the size of her dress, I could see she was a large woman, and by the texture, I knew she cared more about the feel of a dress than about fashion or style. She liked to dress simply and comfortably. I felt guilty in her dress, but it gave me a better sense of Gladys Presley: a woman, as Grandma had described her, with a heart of gold—yet you never wanted to cross her. When she was angry, "she cussed like a sailor and had the wrath of God in her."

I felt sad—for Elvis, for Gladys, for us all—because we have to contend with death. Life could be so different if Gladys were here, I thought, weeping as though she were my own mother. I felt Gladys's presence in that little room, also her grief and loneliness. Maybe it was her spirit that Grandma and Hattie sensed.

All of a sudden, Hattie's face appeared in the doorway. We both screamed with fright, yelling, "What are *you* doing up here?"

"Child, this ain't no place you should be. Too many sad memories. B'sides, it's dark and scary. Only reason I come up is 'cause Miss Minnie was worried 'bout you."

Then, as Hattie walked away, waving her hands above her head, she said under her breath, "No ma'am, I don't like it up here."

21

THE NEXT TIME Elvis returned to Los Angeles, where he was to begin filming *Kissin' Cousins*, I flew with him. I loved L.A. It was exciting compared to the slow pace I had grown accustomed to in Memphis. Best of all, I felt a part of Elvis's world. His hectic schedule and daily life were realities to me now, no longer just remote events chronicled in our nightly phone calls.

The problem was that his life still included Ann-Margret, despite the fact that their film, *Viva Las Vegas*, had been completed six weeks before. The newspapers were reporting their "blossoming" affair daily, each article hitting me like a slap in the face. I thought, When will this be over—the news, the gossip, the headlines, the affair?

Elvis returned from the studio one afternoon, carrying

a newspaper and fuming. "I can't believe she did it." He flung the paper against the wall in disgust. "She had the goddamn nerve to announce we're engaged."

Though I was pretty sure of the answer, I asked, "Who?"

"Ann-Margret. Every major newspaper in America's picked it up. The rumor's spread like a goddamn disease."

Turning to me, he said, "Honey, I'm gonna have to ask you to leave. The press will be hanging around the gate and following me all over for a statement. Colonel suggests maybe you should go back to Memphis till it calms down."

I couldn't believe what I was hearing. Suddenly all the months of unbearable silence broke and I screamed, "What's going on here? I'm tired of these secrets. Telephone calls. Notes. Newspapers!" I picked up a flower vase and hurled it across the room, shattering it against the wall. "I hate her!" I shouted. "Why doesn't she keep her ass in Sweden where she belongs?"

Elvis grabbed me and threw me on the bed. "Look, goddamn it! I didn't know this was going to get out of hand. I want a woman who's going to understand that things like this might just happen." He gave me a hard, penetrating look. "Are you going to be her—or not?"

I stared back at him, furious and defiant, hating him for what he was putting me through.

After a long pause, our tempers cooled considerably. Once again desperate to please, I said, "I'll leave tomorrow. I'll be waiting in Memphis."

Elvis joined me two weeks later. Little was said on the

night of his return. We exchanged forced smiles. Luckily, there were a lot of familiar faces around and this helped disguise the awkwardness of the moment.

After everyone left, Elvis and I finally had to face each other. He walked up to me, took my face in his hands, looked into my eyes, and said, "It's over, Cilla. I swear to you. It's over."

I didn't speak. I just listened carefully as he continued. "I guess I got caught up in a situation that was out of hand from the beginning. She and I come from two different worlds. I don't like being exploited. I can't live like that. Don't get me wrong. She's a nice girl, but not for me."

I didn't want to hear any more. I looked up at him, half-listening to what he was saying and at the same time asking myself how I could go on, knowing that the future would bring only more temptations for him. Love was much more complicated than I had ever imagined.

The silence between the two of us continued until Elvis had had enough and said, "Let's forget it. Forgive me, please." Then, with that little-boy look that always seemed to capture my heart, he said, using Flip Wilson's favorite Geraldine line, "I guess the devil made me do it!"

I agreed.

I would be a little more skeptical now.

And there was still one more matter to take care of. I walked into his bathroom, went through his makeup kit, and pulled out a telegram I knew he'd received earlier. It simply read, I JUST DON'T UNDERSTAND—SCOOBIE. It was from Ann-Margret. I knew it. Scoobie was a name she had given herself, he confessed later. That line was also the title of the first hit record she'd recorded in the early sixties. Obviously, Elvis had totally disassociated himself from her, cutting off their ties.

"It bothers me knowing it's there," I said. I simply tore it to shreds and with total gratification flushed it down the toilet.

"Not too much goes by you, does it, Little One? For such a little girl, you're a typical woman." He was laughing. "I guess I've got to keep on my toes."

I returned his smile but thought: No, I'm the one who has to keep on her toes. A mutual friendship and professional respect between Elvis and Ann-Margret would continue until his death.

After the ordeal with Ann-Margret, I still suspected that there were other women.

Occasionally I'd read or hear about Elvis romancing his latest leading lady. I'd see press-released pictures of them riding down Sunset Boulevard on his new motorcycle or hear about a new car he'd bought for a young starlet just before they'd started shooting a picture. There was always room for doubt. It was difficult to differentiate between gossip and fact, and I'd get crazed with worry.

Before I started traveling with Elvis on a permanent basis, I discovered notes and cards tucked away on a shelf in his closet, notes that read, "I had a wonderful time, Honey, thanks for the evening." Or, "When are we going to get together again? It's been two days, and I miss you." When I voiced my suspicions, he denied everything and accused me of "imagining things." He told me I was ridiculous for believing the gossip columnists. Yet I couldn't help remembering that he'd told me the same thing when I'd asked him about Ann-Margret.

If I really challenged him, I always ran the risk of his threatening to send me home to my parents. He knew this tactic always worked. The first time it happened, he was filming *Spinout* and we were talking about his co-star, Shelley Fabares. I suggested going to the set and meeting her.

"It'd be a good idea if you didn't," he said.

"Why not? I'm not doing anything. I could come and have lunch with you."

I'd obviously said the wrong thing. He shot me a menacing look and said quietly, "That's it, woman! I don't want to hear another word."

It was foolish of me, but I didn't heed his warning. "Well," I persisted, "is there something you're hiding that you don't want me to see?" He flew into a rage.

"I don't have a goddamn thing to hide. You're getting a little too aggressive and demanding. It might be a good idea if you visited your parents for a while."

Shocked, I yelled, "Well I'm not going!"

"I think you should. In fact, I'll help you." He walked over to my closet and proceeded to throw every piece of clothing I had on the floor, hangers included, along with my suitcase on top of the clothes.

"All right, woman. Start packing!"

I couldn't believe this overreaction. It was one of four things: He was innocent, or I had made him feel guilty, or he was guilty, and I'd made him feel even more so, or it was simply his ongoing disgust with the inane plot of the film and he'd chosen me as a target for his anger.

Sobbing, I started to pack as he turned and strode out of the room. Moments later I heard him yelling for Joe to make a reservation. "Get her on the next flight out. She's going back to her parents." There was a finality in his voice that I had never heard before. Hysterical, I began folding my clothes as he continued yelling in the other room. I packed slowly, stunned by the blowup.

When he came back into the room, I felt humiliated. I continued folding clothes, sobbing uncontrollably. "You're too goddamn demanding," he said, staring at me in silence. "Hurry up. It's time to go."

I got up slowly and started toward the door. Just as I reached it, I felt his hand on my shoulder, turning me around, and then, miraculously, I was in his arms, and he was holding me tight.

"Now do you understand?" As he spoke, I was sobbing against his shoulder. "Do you see that you need this? You need someone to take you right to this point and put you in your place."

I was relieved and happy to be back in his arms. Anything he'd have said would've made sense to me in that moment. What I didn't realize until later was that this was Elvis's technique of keeping me under control.

22

I'D NOW BEEN living with Elvis about two years and traveling with him regularly. My parents, having returned from Germany, were now staying temporarily with my Uncle Ray in Connecticut, on their way to Travis Air Force Base near Sacramento. I was anxious to see them, yet I hated leaving Graceland. Outside those gates, the cord was cut. I was afraid that the one moment I was away from his world would be the one moment when another could slip in.

Yet I needed to see my parents. I did miss them. I was well aware that my appearance—in a tight, form-fitting dress, spiked high heels, heavy makeup, and with my hair dyed jet black and piled high on top of my head in a beehive hairdo—would elicit, as usual, a less than delighted response from them, but I was determined not to change a single part of the total look that Elvis had painstakingly created. I flew to Connecticut and my expectations were correct. My parents were again so shocked when they saw me that they could barely speak. Later, my father told me that under all that makeup, my eyes looked like "two pissholes in the snow."

The rest of the weekend brought no improvement. I wasn't being honest about my relationship and style of life. Anticipating uncomfortable questions about my future, I spent most of the time in my room. However, the questions came.

"What's it like, living at Graceland?"

"Is it true that Elvis never goes anywhere?"

I felt their probing was an invasion of my privacy, my personal life, and I gave them guarded answers.

My parents didn't appreciate my attitude or my defensiveness. They were just showing a natural interest in me, and a concern for my well-being, when they asked how I'd done in school, what kinds of grades I'd gotten, and if I'd brought my report card. They also wanted to know if I was planning to attend college. Even though my only plan was to go wherever Elvis was going, I said that I intended to enroll. I tried to tell them what they wanted to hear, and to say as little as possible, convinced that if I said one thing wrong, they'd order me home.

After that weekend, I tried to avoid my parents. But they knew I joined Elvis in Los Angeles while he was filming, and they wanted me to spend weekends with them in Sacramento. This created a problem. I couldn't think of sharing my time with anyone but Elvis, especially weekends when he wasn't working. Still,

I'd make occasional trips to Sacramento, because if I didn't visit my parents, they'd visit us. I knew Elvis was very touchy, and I was never sure what might set him off.

I was particularly nervous when my parents decided to bring my sister and brothers down to Disneyland for the weekend—and to stop and see us in Bel Air. I persuaded them that Bel Air was much too far out of their way and it'd be easier for me to meet them at Disneyland. I spent the weekend with them there, but on Sunday my parents insisted on bringing me home. Of course I had to invite them all to dinner.

They dropped me off and drove on to a nearby hotel to check in and get changed. I ran into the house in a panic because I knew I'd have to show them around. I certainly couldn't tell my parents that I slept with Elvis, and I decided to try to fool them into believing that I had my own room.

I asked Charlie Hodge, one of the employees, if I could borrow his room. I rushed up and down the hall, taking things from Elvis's room and putting them in Charlie's. I placed my little perfume bottles around the tables, hung some of my clothes in the closet, which I strategically left partly open, and finally put all of the stuffed dogs and teddy bears that I loved to collect on the bed.

That evening when we had dinner, Elvis was charming and wonderful, but I was too petrified to eat. I was always anxious whenever Elvis and my father got together, since I never knew what Dad was going to ask him. Elvis used to get very annoyed because so many people were curious about the "regulars," always asking what this one did, or that one did, and why Elvis needed to have so many of them around him. When I would try and tell Dad to be less curious, that only made him *more* curious.

"Why can't I ask questions?" he'd demand. "What's there to hide?"

After dinner, I gave my family a tour of the house. I tried to show them "my" room as casually as I had the others. "See how it overlooks the patio," I said calmly. "Come on, I'll show you Elvis's room."

I opened the door to his room, praying that no one would want to see any of his huge walk-in closets because if they opened a closet door, all of my things would be revealed. One of my shoes, I noticed in horror, had been left next to the bed. I managed to kick it out of sight.

Amazingly, the entire evening came off without mishap. Although my parents never questioned the story about my own room, I'm sure they never believed it either.

That night, when Elvis looked in Charlie's room and saw all of the stuffed animals, he burst out laughing.

I continued to guard my life-style. I was always afraid they'd look too closely at my relationship with Elvis. As it was, they inquired about our future together.

"How much longer is this going to go on like this?" they wanted to know. "What are his intentions? Are there any plans for anything? If not, why don't you just pack your bags and come home? We think it's about time."

Hearing this was my greatest fear. I always told them, "We're doing great. I'm sure everything will work out fine." I'd give them vanilla ice cream with candy and whipped cream and a cherry on top—so that everything sounded really promising.

23

EVERYTHING WASN'T NEARLY as promising as I led my parents to believe. Elvis and I couldn't really be happy together because he was so unhappy with his career. At first glance, he had it made: He was the highest-paid actor in Hollywood with a three-picture-a-year contract, at a phenomenal salary, plus fifty percent of the profits. But in reality, his brilliant career had lost its luster. By 1965 the public had access to Elvis solely through his films and records. He hadn't appeared on television since his special with Frank Sinatra in 1960, and he hadn't performed in a live concert since the spring of 1961.

The sales of his records indicated that his massive popularity was slipping. His singles were no longer automatically Top Ten hits, and he hadn't enjoyed a Number One record since the spring of 1962.

He blamed his fading popularity on his humdrum

movies. He loathed their stock plots and short shooting schedules, but whenever he complained to the Colonel, Colonel reminded him that they were making millions, that the fact that his last two serious films, *Flaming Star* and *Wild in the Country*, were box-office failures proved that his fans wanted to see him only in musicals.

He could have demanded better, more substantial scripts but he didn't. Part of the reason was the lavish life-style he had established and become accustomed to. The main reason, however, was his inability to stand up to the Colonel. In Elvis's personal life, there were no stops in letting anyone know how or what he felt. But when it came time to stand up to Colonel Parker, he backed off. Elvis detested the business side of his career. He would sign a contract without even reading it.

He was an artist to whom the act of creation was everything. He and the Colonel had an unwritten agreement: Elvis would handle the artistic end and the Colonel would take care of business matters. This resulted in the Colonel locking Elvis into one bad picture after another. The Colonel's view was, if they were a success in the past, why change the trend?

Elvis was also becoming disillusioned with his music. Although he'd never had a lesson in his life, he was brilliant musically, and he loved all kinds of music—gospel, opera, rhythm and blues, country, and rock. The only kind of music he wasn't terribly fond of was jazz.

For years Elvis had stayed on top of the record charts because he had been given a good selection of songs to choose from, and he'd had free rein to record them in his own style, his own way, and had not yet become disillusioned with the music industry.

In the studio, Elvis worked well with people he felt comfortable with, and he knew exactly what sound he wanted. He handpicked his musicians and backup singers, and if he liked their sound, his own voice would reach new heights. He loved blending voices, and he marveled at the range of the tenor and bass singers. During a session, he'd stop recording, walk over to the backup singers, and harmonize the songs with them, laughing and joking and daring each one to go higher or lower, seeing if he could keep in their range. Most of the time, when he was vocally in shape, he could, and did.

When he was excited about the material, he loved recording sessions. He liked to work as a team—with his voice, the backup singers, and the instruments all recorded at the same volume. He didn't want his voice out front alone. He liked the impact of the whole group. It was his sound, and it was a fabulous sound until one day Colonel said there were complaints from fans and from RCA that they couldn't hear Elvis well enough. Whether or not this was true, he suggested Elvis's voice be brought out more.

This is one of the few times Elvis bucked heads with him, stating, "I've been singing that way all of my life. What do a few heads in RCA know about music? I'll sing the songs the way I hear them."

The recording engineer, however, worked not for Elvis but for RCA, and he began pulling back the group.

"The old man's tampering with my soundtracks," he complained to Red West and me in the back of the limo on our way to the Memphian one evening. "I don't have a chance in hell. RCA's listening to him. Fans aren't gonna want to hear my goddamn voice out front. Hell, that's what my style was all about. You could hardly understand me. Made you want to listen. And the songs that are hits today—you can hardly make out what they're singin'. The man should stick to his deals, keep out of my goddamn affairs."

Elvis could handle only so much and then he'd lose heart. He'd put up with the horrendous movies, but now they were tampering with his songs.

Colonel did not intentionally plot to make Elvis sound bad, or to get artistic control. His only interest was in getting out the product so the money could keep coming in. But when he started crossing over the line from business negotiations into Elvis's artistry, Elvis slowly began going downhill.

I wanted desperately to help him, but I wasn't sure how. In my innocence, I kept trying to convince him to argue with the Colonel. But he would only get angry, saying I didn't know what I was talking about.

I didn't understand his difficulty in revealing his weaknesses to me. Only later did I realize how important it was to Elvis to always appear in control in front of me. Whenever I stated my own opinions too strongly, especially if they differed from his, he'd remind me that his was the stronger sex, and as a woman, I had my place. He liked to say that it was intended for woman to be on the left side of man, close to his heart, where she gives him strength through her support.

His role with me was that of lover and father, and with neither could he let down his guard and become fallible or truly intimate. I longed for that, and as a woman, I needed it.

There were nights when he slept restlessly, beset by

worries and fears. I lay silently beside him, anxious about what he might be thinking and whether there was a place in his life for me. Lost in our separate miseries, we were unable to give each other strength or support. He was controlled by his inability to take responsibility for his own life and for compromising his own standards—and I was controlled by him, compromising mine.

When things were bad, Elvis called Vernon and they talked for hours about their problems. He told his daddy he was lonely and depressed and no one understood him. When I overheard these words, I continued to take it personally, again thinking that I was failing him.

I would put on my brightest smile, my prettiest dress—and my phoniest personality—and try to rouse his spirits. When I couldn't get him out of the dumps, he would shut himself up all day in his room. This left me devastated. Afraid of saying or doing the wrong thing, I suppressed my real feelings and eventually developed an ulcer.

The more frustrations increased, the more pressure he felt and this resulted in his manifesting physical illnesses. Specifically to handle depression, he was now prescribed antidepressants. His enormously creative gifts were being squandered and he couldn't face it.

Although Colonel Parker knew about his state of mind, he had a long-standing agreement with Elvis that he'd stay out of his personal life. Instead of confronting Elvis, he tried to get the guys to report to him. It was a very touchy situation, and the boys were skeptical. Colonel used to have Sonny West and Jerry Schilling drive him back and forth to Palm Springs on weekends. During the long drive he casually tried to pump them for information. They had to be very careful. If they said the wrong thing, they would be put in a position of having betrayed Elvis.

It was especially hard on Joe Esposito who, as foreman of the group, spent a lot of time with the Colonel. When Elvis began canceling meetings, or acting strangely on the set, Colonel would say, "What's going on with Elvis, Joe? He looks like he's in bad shape. We can't let him be seen like this."

Joe was torn between his loyalties to Colonel and to Elvis. He cared about Elvis and respected his wishes, but he understood that the Colonel made the deals and had to deliver "the product": Elvis.

When Colonel made Joe responsible for reporting to him on Elvis's "mental and emotional state," a euphemistic phrase for drug use, Elvis found out and said, "I don't want any sons of bitches here telling Colonel what I do or what goes on in this household." He fired Joe on the spot. Six months later he forgave him and took him back. It was typical of Elvis to blow off steam and then forgive all.

From the time I first arrived at Graceland I began to notice a gradual change in Elvis's personality. In the early days of our relationship he seemed to be more in command of his emotions.

He was a man capable of enjoying life to the fullest, especially during our own special times. We loved to stroll about in the early evenings just before dark. Usually we'd end up at his father's home and stay and watch television, father and son relaxing, puffing on cigars, discussing the state of the world.

Frequently the subject was Vernon's intention to trade in his car, an elaborate Cadillac Elvis had given him, for a 1950 Olds he felt far more comfortable driving. Vernon loved old cars and trucks, trading them every few months, delighted with each new deal.

Walking back home with Elvis, we'd speak of fate—how it had brought us together, how we were meant for each other, how God worked in strange ways, uniting two people from different parts of the world.

I loved it when he'd talk like this. He'd plan our lives, saying how he was destined to be with me and could never be with anyone else. In this loving atmosphere I found I could open up and express my opinions freely.

I look back now and realize that our love affair was dependent on how his career was going. During protracted periods of noncreativity, his temper often flared.

Once we were going through a stack of demo records for an RCA soundtrack album and his distaste for each song grew increasingly apparent. Before a record was halfway through, he was on to the next, getting more and more discouraged. Finally he found one that held his attention and asked me what I thought. Remembering that first incident in Vegas, I truly felt our relationship had developed to where he would want my honest opinion. "I don't really like it," I said.

"What do you mean, you don't like it?"

"I don't know—there's just something about it, a catchiness that's missing."

To my horror, a chair came hurtling toward me.

I moved out of the way just in time, but there were stacks of records piled on it and one flew off and hit me in the face.

Within seconds he had me in his arms, apologizing frantically. It was said that he inherited his temper from his parents. I'd heard stories about how, when Gladys was furious, she'd grab a frying pan and fling it at Vernon, and I'd already observed Vernon's harsh words firsthand. This genetic trait was inherent in Elvis's temperament.

You could sense the vibration when he was angry. The tension in the room mounted to flash point, and no one wanted to be around for the explosion. Yet, if anyone decided to leave, they automatically became the target for his rage, me included. Like the time he came storming downstairs because his black suit—which he had worn only the day before—hadn't been returned from the cleaners.

"Why isn't it back yet, Cilla?" he screamed. "Where the hell is my goddamn suit?"

He had two other suits identical to the one at the cleaners, but he wanted *that* one.

When he was angry, it was like the roar of thunder. No one could challenge his biting words; we could only wait until the storm passed. When he calmed down, he made excuses—he hadn't had enough sleep, he'd had too much sleep, or he hadn't had his morning coffee yet.

Sometimes he lashed out just to drive home a point. If he thought it would teach us a lesson, he'd blow some minor grievance out of all proportion, and even as he was yelling he might wink at someone nearby. Then, ten minutes later, he'd be fine, leaving us bewildered and emotionally depleted. There were also times he would leave us emotionally uplifted. He was truly a master at manipulating people.

24

ELVIS WAS FILLED with complexities and contradictions. We would spend an evening discussing the spiritual life and then watch horror films.

One evening while watching the classic horror movie *Diabolique*, Elvis leaned over and asked if I was in a daring mood.

"Sure." I didn't know what he was up to, but adventure excited me.

"I'm going to take you somewhere that will scare the *fire* out of you—it did me the first time I went there."

After the film he took my hand and we all piled into the limo. Elvis instructed the driver, "Take us to the Memphis morgue."

"What!"

I didn't believe what I had just heard.

"Yeah, there's this guy who oversees the place. I went

there once before. I was roaming around the rooms, looking at bodies, and we ran into each other. It scared the shit out of us both."

"You mean we're going *inside?*"

"Well, we're not supposed to, but I got ways."

"Okay, I'm game."

His fame was his passkey. It was eerie walking through the halls and viewing each room. They were still, solemn, dimly lit. I clutched at Elvis's hand. At first I didn't want to look, but he assured me the bodies were at peace and that once I looked, it wouldn't be so bad.

We wandered from room to room. I was amazed at how easy it was to become accustomed to this unusual sight. It was serene, almost as if we were in church.

We were doing fine until I looked on a table and saw an infant who appeared to be two or three months old. We both gazed in silence.

"Oh Sattnin," I said, "he's so little, so innocent. What could have happened? There's no scars." Tears were streaming down my face.

"I don't know," he said softly. "Sometimes God works in strange ways. I guess it was just meant for the little fellow to be with Him."

We both took the infant's hand and Elvis said a prayer. A few minutes later, we stood over a middle-aged woman who had just been embalmed. I looked away.

"This is good for you," he said. "You have to see things like this sometimes. This is the hard cold fact— reality. When you look at a body, you realize how temporary it all is, how it could end in a matter of minutes."

The spiritual side of Elvis was a dominant part of his nature. As a small boy growing up in Tupelo, Mississippi, he and his family attended church regularly at the First Assembly of God. He was raised on hellfire-and-brimstone preaching that put the fear of God in you and music that led to the Pearly Gates. Elvis, Vernon, and Gladys would join in with the congregation and choir, and it was then that music first rocked Elvis's soul. He was capable of spiritual healing; one touch of his hands to my temples and the most painful headaches disappeared.

He always kept the Bible on his bedside table and read it often. Now, faced with an ever-deepening despair, he began looking to other philosophical books for answers and guidance. He read the works of Kahlil Gibran. One book in particular, *The Prophet*, inspired him. He also read *Siddhartha* by Hermann Hesse and *The Impersonal Life* by Joseph Benner. He became so enamored of these books that he passed them out to friends, fellow actors, and fans. They appealed to his religious nature and he loved bringing people together "in the spirit of one underlying force—Almighty God."

When his mother, Gladys, was alive, Elvis had one person to answer to, whom he respected and who constantly reminded him of his values and his roots. It was Gladys who kept Elvis aware of the difference between right and wrong, of the evils of temptation, and of the danger of life in the fast lane.

"Mama," he'd say. "I want you and Daddy in Hollywood with me. There's a lot of fast-talkin' businessmen there, makin' a lot of decisions, fancy talk I don't understand."

In the early days, Vernon and Gladys accompanied Elvis on most of his major appearances around the South and visits to Hollywood when he made his first films. It was Gladys's common sense that counteracted Elvis's insecurities in his youth.

Since Gladys's death, there were no boundaries for Elvis. She was the force that kept him in line. Now that she was gone, he was continually in conflict between his own personal ethics and the temptations that surrounded him.

By the mid-sixties he was holding Bible readings in the den of our Bel Air home. I sat next to him one evening as he read passages with great force. Facing us were several of his young female admirers wearing the lowest-cut blouses and the shortest miniskirts. They all listened attentively, disciples enraptured in the presence of "their" lord. The sermon stretched to hours, followed by a question-and-answer period during which they vied for his attention.

Sitting at his feet was an attractive, well-endowed young girl wearing a blouse unbuttoned to her navel. Leaning over seductively, she asked in honeyed tones, "Elvis, do you think the woman at the well was a virgin?" With me right beside him, he avoided taking in the fleshy spectacle obviously exposed for his benefit.

"Well, honey," he said, "that's somethin' you'll have to come to a conclusion on yourself. As for me, I personally think Jesus was attracted to her, but that's my opinion. I'm not sayin' it's fact."

I watched Elvis and the girl talking, feeling undermined and angry. How stupid, I thought. Can't he see what she's doing? It's so obvious.

He drew in a deep breath and said, "I like your perfume, honey. What's it called?"

"Chanel Number Five," she answered.

Chanel Number Five? That's what *I* was wearing! Why didn't he notice it on me? I slowly rose and walked into my dressing room adjacent to the den. Determined to snare his attention, I changed into his favorite outfit—a tight-fitting black sheath he had picked out himself.

Returning a few minutes later, I took my place beside him, but he was wrapped up in preaching to his devotees and had totally overlooked my absence. To make matters worse, he didn't even notice my change of costume. I managed to conceal my distress behind a fake smile and an attentive gaze, but I couldn't help noticing that he was responding to them with an occasional wink or smile.

I asked questions like they did, but my heart wasn't in it; I knew they all wanted to take my place. "That's it," I thought. "If I'm not appreciated, loved, or wanted, I'll end it. That will make it easier for everyone."

I got up and went back to our room. Picking up a half-full bottle of Placidyls, I devised a plan to create a dramatic effect that, in my mind, would win his attention. I stared at them, thinking, What if I choke to death? I decided to take two pills to start. That way I could take a quick shower, redo my makeup, put on my prettiest camisole, and still have time to position myself dramatically on the bed before I consumed the rest of the bottle.

I swallowed the pills and started to prepare myself for the end. In tears, I thought of leaving him a note, writing down everything I'd never been able to say. I'd tell him how I wished that it could have been just the two of us again, as it had been during the long hours we'd spent together in his room in Germany. I'd confess that I was jealous of any woman who caught his attention and that I hated the times when there was only silence between us, even though he'd said he had things on his mind. I'd tell him how I feared his violent temper, which robbed me of my freedom of expression; and how I wished that he'd have tried to understand me as I'd desperately tried to understand him.

Maybe he's missed me by now, I thought. I ran to the door and pressed my ear against it. I heard him laughing. He was having a great time. They all were.

I found that I was disgusted with all of it. I wouldn't go in there now if he begged me, I told myself. I was too tired anyway.

But I wasn't too tired to remember how I wanted to be found. I lay down on the bed with my long jet black hair spread over the white pillows, my lips moist with gloss. In my naive fantasy he'd take my listless body in his arms and tell me how much he loved me, kissing me passionately back to life.

I forced down one more pill, lay perfectly still in the position I wanted to be discovered, and waited for what seemed like hours for sleep to overtake me. But the longer I lay there, the less sleepy I became. The more I heard Elvis's laughter, the angrier I got. My adrenaline-charged fury was overriding the effect of the pills. Soon I began to feel foolish.

Then I heard Elvis say good night to everyone as he approached the room. I grabbed the nearest book and lay it at my side, as though I'd been reading and had fallen asleep. I heard him come in, quietly walk over to the bed, and pick up the book. He whispered the title, *The Listener*. I could imagine him smiling, pleased as always when I read philosophical books. He stood over me for a second, probably thinking how sweet I looked and how tired I must have been to retire so early.

Then he covered me snugly with blankets and bent down to kiss my carefully-parted lips. All my anger and jealously vanished. I realized how even a little of his attention could make me happy.

25

In April of 1964, Larry Geller was hired to replace
Elvis's barber, Sal Orfice. Little did we know that their
relationship would not only cause a drastic change in
Elvis, but it would create tension, jealousy, and fear
within the group.

I was in Memphis when he first met Larry, but I
learned all about him through our nightly phone conversations. Elvis's enthusiasm over his newfound friend was
infectious.

"You're not going to believe this guy, Sattnin," he
said. "Larry knows more about the spiritual world than
all the preachers and Catholic priests and religious fanat-
ics put together. We have discussions that last hours, just
nd talkin' about the great masters and my pur-

pose for being here. I'm invitin' him to Graceland. He'll enlighten your spiritual development."

When Larry and his wife, Stevie Geller, joined us, I was surprised to find them both young and attractive. He was kind and mellow. She was sweet and quiet and kept to herself.

However, many in the group, myself included, were suspicious of them. We were all threatened by Elvis's involvement with Larry. It was keeping him from us. It seemed as if Elvis was always off alone reading esoteric books or deep in discussion with Larry about God's master plan for the universe.

Elvis discovered there were many great masters besides Jesus. There were Buddha, Muhammad, Moses, and others, each "chosen by God to serve a purpose." What I was now witnessing in Elvis was the emergence of that part of his nature that was thirsting for answers to all the fundamental questions of life.

He asked Larry why, out of all the people in the universe, he had been chosen to influence so many millions of souls. Granted this unique position, how could he contribute to save a world burdened with hunger, disease, and poverty? Why was there so much human suffering in the first place? And why wasn't he happy, when he had more than anyone could want? He felt he was missing something in life. Through Larry's insight, he hoped to find the path that would lead him to the answers.

He was eager for all of us—especially me—to absorb all the knowledge he was consuming. Happy to share everything, just as he had with his Bible discussions in

L.A., he read to us for hours and handed out books he thought would interest us. He announced that in order for us to be perfect soul mates, I'd have to join him in his search for the answers to the universe. To help me, he gave me several large books, including Vera Stanley Adler's *The Initiation of the World.*

He suggested I attend the lectures of the metaphysical philosopher and author Manley P. Hall. I did. I found the lectures difficult to understand and painful to endure, but I managed to survive with the hope that "this too shall pass."

Then he became interested in Cheiro's *Book of Numbers,* which defined people's personality traits and characteristics according to the day of the month on which they were born. To find out who was compatible with whom, Elvis added up the numbers in the birthdays of everyone within the group. I waited in terror, praying that my number would be a six, seven, or eight, so I would be compatible with Elvis, who was an eight. Fortunately, my number linked with his.

Although I was striving to be his soul mate and subtly becoming more aware of myself as a spiritual being, my heart longed for the very temptations he was fighting to conquer.

While I patiently waited at home at Graceland for his returns, planning romantic interludes, he was attempting to overcome worldly temptations and believed he was going through a cleansing period, physically and spiritually. Any sexual temptations were against everything he was striving for, and he did not wish to betray me, the girl waiting for him at home who was preparing to be his wife.

He felt guilty and confused about his natural reaction to female advances and I believe that this was his greatest fear when it came to marriage. He loved me and deeply wanted to be faithful to me but never felt certain that he could resist temptation. It was a persistent battle, and it even got to the point where he felt he had to resist me.

"Cilla," he said one night before we went to bed, "you're going to have to be pretty understanding these next few weeks, or however long it takes. I feel that I have to withdraw myself from the temptations of sex."

"But why? And why with me?"

He was quite solemn. "We have to control our desires so they don't control us. If we can control sex, then we can master all other desires."

When we were in bed, he took his usual dose of sleeping pills, handed me mine, and then, fighting off drowsiness from the pills, pored over his metaphysical books.

As his soul mate I was expected to search for answers as fervently as he did, but I just couldn't bear reading the ponderous tracts that surrounded us in bed every night. Usually within five minutes of opening one, I'd be sound asleep. Annoyed at my obvious disinterest, he woke me to share an insightful passage. If I voiced the slightest protest, he'd say, "Things will never work out between us, Cilla, because you don't show any interest in me or my philosophies." Then, pointedly: "There are a lot of women out there who would share these things with me."

Faced with this threat, I forced myself to sit up and try to read the passage. The print swam before my eyes in one big blur.

I wanted to share romantic, not religious, inspirations with him. I tried to cuddle as close to him as I could, feeling the warmth of his body. He told me to sit up and listen, and he read yet another passage, repeating it several times to make sure I grasped its significance. I could bear it no longer. I lost control and started screaming.

"I can't stand it! I don't want to hear any more! I'm sick and tired of your voice going on and *on*! It's—driving—me—crazy!" I was hysterical, pulling at my hair like a wild woman.

"What do you see?" I demanded. "*Tell* me, what do you see?"

He stared up at me, his eyes half-closed. "A madwoman, a goddamn raving madwoman," he answered, slurring his words because of the sleeping pills.

I fell on my knees beside him, crying, "No, Elvis, not a madwoman, a woman who needs to make love to and to feel desired by her man. Elvis, you can have your books and me too. Please don't make me beg," I cried. "I really need you and want you."

By the time I'd finished my tirade, all I could hear was the faint sound of religious music playing on the radio. I looked up at him. He had fallen into a deep sleep.

26

ELVIS WAS NOT one for moderation. Whether it was motorcycles, slot cars, horses, amusement parks, roller skating, sex, or even eating the same dinner day after day, if he enjoyed it, he'd overindulge.

One evening I gave him a little racetrack with remote-control cars. A few weeks later he had an entire room added onto the house with a professional game track. There he played night after night until he had his fill and then he never went back to the room until much later, when the annex was converted into a trophy room filled with his gold records and awards.

As Elvis's fascination with occult and metaphysical phenomena intensified, Larry introduced him to the Self-Realization Fellowship Center on Mount Washington, where he met Daya Mata, the head of the center. She was an attractive woman who looked remarkably like Gladys Presley, and he was captivated by her serenity and spiritual presence. She epitomized everything he was striving to be.

He made several trips to Mount Washington, high in the Hollywood Hills, for sessions with Daya Mata in the hope of attaining *kriya*, which is the highest form of meditation in the self-realization fellowship. He was especially intrigued by Paramahansa Yogananda, the center's deceased founder and author of *The Autobiography of a Yogi*.

He read that Yogananda had reached such a high state of consciousness that his spirit could control his body even after death. Yogananda's body lay in an open casket at Forest Lawn Cemetery for over twenty days without showing any signs of decomposition. It was this kind of higher state of consciousness that Elvis was hoping to achieve.

As relaxed and peaceful as he was upon leaving the center's hushed grounds, one thing he couldn't pass up was a good fight. We were on our way home from Mount Washington one afternoon when our limousine passed a service station where two attendants were staging a fight.

"Pull over," Elvis ordered the driver. "Someone's in trouble."

He jumped out of the car, Jerry and Sonny following

him. Going up to one of the men, he said, "Hey, you want to give somebody trouble, give it to me."

"Hey man," the guy answered, scarcely able to believe this was Elvis. "I don't have any problem with you. I'm not arguing with you."

"I'll show you something, if you want to get into an argument," Elvis said. He shot out a karate kick, and to his surprise—and everyone else's—he knocked a pack of cigarettes out of the guy's pocket. Among our group, Elvis wasn't known for his precision in karate.

Long after the service station fracas, we joked about it, saying, "Man, the Lord had to be on E's side that day. That guy doesn't know how lucky he was."

Of course Elvis had acted as if he could do this any time he felt like it. After executing that kick he'd walked away with a cocky smile, warning the guy to stay out of trouble or there'd be more where that had come from.

When we got home, the way Elvis told it you'd think he'd just wiped out half a battalion. We all supported his fantasy.

He was eagerly looking forward to one particular film, *Harum Scarum*, seeing it as a chance to create a genuinely interesting character. He identified his role with Rudolph Valentino's in *The Sheik*. At last, he thought, a part he could sink his teeth into. He saw a physical resemblance between himself and Valentino, especially in profile.

During preproduction, he came home darkened with makeup, dressed in white harem pants and a white turban. He looked extremely handsome, much more so than Valentino, I thought. Tilting his head down, with a piercing gaze and flared nostrils, he asked rhetorically, "Frightening, isn't it, how much I look like him? How does this get to ya?" He took me in his arms Valentino-style and dipped me over à la the famous poster of the Sheik.

Night after night he kept his makeup and the turban on all through dinner and up until bedtime.

Although he was excited about the film when he first started shooting, as each day went by, his morale plummeted. *Harum Scarum*'s plot was a joke, the character he played, a fool, and the songs he sang, disasters. The film turned out to be yet another disappointment, an embarrassing one at that.

Still committed to the picture but demeaned by its mediocrity, he sought escape on his motorbikes—eleven Triumphs and a Harley—a Triumph for each assistant and a Harley for the boss. Decked out in leather from head to toe and feeling as tough as a pack of Hell's Angels on a rampage, we roared through the gates of Bel Air, revving our engines at all hours of the night.

Weekends we took trips through the Santa Monica Mountains, stopping off for beer or cola along the way. It was fast, fun, and wild. I liked it so much I wanted my own bike. Despite his concern for my safety, Elvis reluctantly bought me a Honda Dream 350.

While he was at the studio I sometimes rode alone,

fleeing Bel Air, Beverly Hills, Hollywood, MGM, and all my worries.

During this period when he was still seeking "a higher state of consciousness," we experimented with mind-expanding drugs. We tried marijuana a few times and neither of us especially liked it. We felt tired and groggy and we'd become ravenously hungry. After a few raids on the refrigerator—and carrying the resulting extra poundage—we decided to stay away from the stuff.

Although he abhorred street drugs he was curious enough to try LSD once. When he initiated our experiment, he made sure Sonny West was on hand at all times to supervise. The night we tried it Lamar, Jerry, Larry, Elvis, and I took seats around the conference table in Elvis's office upstairs at Graceland.

Elvis and I took half a tab. At first, nothing happened. Then we started staring at each other and laughing—our faces were becoming distorted.

I became engrossed in Elvis's multicolored shirt. It started to grow, getting larger and larger until I thought he was going to burst. It was captivating, but I did not like the feeling. I thought: This isn't real, be careful, you're losing it. I tried to hang on to sanity.

We all gathered around the large aquarium outside the master bedroom, fascinated by the tropical fish. Funny—there were only two or three, but suddenly I saw an ocean of brightly colored fish. I strolled off and found myself in Elvis's huge walk-in closet, purring like a kitten.

It was early morning when Elvis and I went downstairs and walked outside. Dew came down, creating rainbows in the mist, glistening on the trees and the lawn. We studied the leaves, trying to count each dewdrop. The veins in the grass became visible, breathing slowly, rhythmically. We went from tree to tree, observing nature in detail.

It was an extraordinary experience. However, realizing it was too dangerous a drug to fool around with, we never tried LSD again.

27

BY 1966, ELVIS'S long search for answers to the mystery of life involved us all in the strange games he loved to devise.

In the backyard of our Bel Air home we found him staring up at "planets moving across the sky" for long periods in the darkness of the early-morning hours. He was convinced, and nearly had us convinced, that there were energy waves so powerful they caused the stars to glide through the universe. For hours we all gazed up in wonderment, questioning each other about what we were seeing, afraid to ask ourselves anything but "Could it be possible?"

His imagination peaked later on when we were all standing in the yard, looking over at the Bel Air Country

Club, which was being watered by a fanlike automatic sprinkler system.

"Do you see them?" said Elvis, looking intently at the course.

"See what?" I asked, ready to hear anything.

"The angels, out there."

"Angels?" I asked, looking down at the sprinklers. I *wanted* to believe him, we all did and we went along with it.

As if in a trance, he continued staring at the water for a few minutes. Then he began moving toward them. "I have to go," he said. "You stay here. They're trying to tell me something." He wandered off toward the golf course in pursuit of his vision. Sonny followed, insuring Elvis's safety, and the rest of us were left dumbfounded.

Other times he'd have us stare for hours at the off-white, nubby-textured ceilings, trying to make out delicately lined faces that he said he was causing to appear.

After his death, some of us have discussed those days, bringing up the possibility of a nervous breakdown—and then discounting it. More likely it was just a game he'd made up out of boredom and depression because he was experiencing such a low point in his career. He took sleeping pills to escape, and while fighting off their effect, he created his "images"—his mystical exercises.

The happiest I ever saw him was when he developed a passion for horses. It all began when I said I wished I had my own horse. I'd loved them since childhood, and Graceland had a beautiful old stable in back, where Vernon used to store old furniture. It was equipped with a tack room, hayloft, and several stalls.

About two weeks later, I was in my dressing room when Elvis, who had been out for a few hours, returned and knocked on my door. "Sattnin, I want you to come downstairs for a minute, got something I want to show you."

He led me down the stairway, his eyes shining. Then he guided me out the back door, his hands over my eyes. When he took them away I saw the most beautiful sight I'd ever laid eyes on—a black quarterhorse with one white stocking.

"His name must be Domino," I said, petting the spirited four-year-old. "Whose is he?"

"He's yours." Elvis was grinning. "I saw this kid riding him, asked if he wanted to sell. I could just picture you on him."

"You mean he's really mine?" I yelled, jumping up and down, throwing my arms around Elvis. I wanted to ride Domino immediately and I mounted him.

"Now, wait a minute," Elvis cautioned. "Don't go off gettin' yourself hurt."

He watched me with a concerned look as I rode out through the pasture and then up to the window of Grandma's room.

"Dodger! Dodger!" I shouted. "Look what I got, my own horse! Isn't he beautiful? Elvis just bought him for me!"

"Good Lord," Dodger cried. "Get off that thing, Priscilla. You're gonna get yourself killed. I'm gonna whop that young'un for gettin' you that. You got no business ridin' that creature."

"It's okay, Dodger, I can handle him," I called out, riding off happily.

He was wild and spirited. When I rode in the late afternoons, I was in my own world. It was a wonderful release. Often Elvis would watch me from his upstairs window. I'd call out to him, "Come down and ride with me."

Elvis didn't ride very well at that time. About the only experience he'd had was in a few of his films, where he didn't feel totally at ease. In fact, he was somewhat intimidated by large animals; nonetheless, he accepted my invitation and tried riding Domino.

He loved it, declaring, "I want a horse of my own, a golden palomino."

Jerry Schilling found Rising Sun at a nearby stable. He was the handsomest palomino imaginable—big and powerful. He'd been trained for shows, and I've never seen an animal that demanded and thrived on as much attention as Rising Sun. There was no doubt that this was the horse for Elvis.

He remained skeptical and had Jerry test Sun out. "Hey, it's beautiful, man," Elvis said. "A great-looking horse. Jerry, you get on it and ride." Jerry had little, if any, riding experience and was horrified at the thought. Nonetheless, he gamely mounted Sun, looking as misplaced as Noël Coward on a Clydesdale.

Sun took off like a bullet with Jerry barely holding on,

every bit of pride in his boots. The magnificent animal seemed to be studying Elvis as much as Elvis was studying him. He raced back, heading straight to where Elvis was standing. "Hold 'em back," Elvis yelled. "I am, E, I am," shouted Jerry. Elvis was won over.

Now we all developed horse fever. We rode late afternoons and well into the evenings. But this wasn't enough for Elvis. As with anything he enjoyed, he wanted everyone else to join the fun. Thus began our quest for horses for the group, including their wives. We bought horses for Billy and Joe Smith, Joe Esposito, Jerry and Sandy Schilling, Lamar, Charlie, Red, Sonny, Richchard—everyone. We bought the finest saddles, blankets, halters, bits, reins, feeding buckets. Anything that had to do with a horse, we bought.

Every afternoon we'd all mount up and ride, in full view of the two hundred or so local fans lined up along the fences. In western riding gear—chaps included—Elvis would turn it into a show. He'd race down the long slope in front of Graceland and then strut back and forth before the fans, demonstrating how well he could ride. He'd have all-out races with the guys as the fans cheered them on.

They were in for even more of a spectacle when Elvis bought his prize black Tennessee Walker, nicknamed Bear, which he rode attired in full show regalia. He and Bear put on a fancy high-stepping show that—if made available to paying customers—would probably have matched his Vegas take.

His other hobbies—go-carts and model cars—were

only machines. This was the first hobby that involved a living creature. The horses responded to his love, and it was touching to witness his attachment to them.

It was a close time for all of us, we had something in common. However, after Elvis had delighted in lavishing horses on all of us, Graceland wasn't quite big enough to handle the herds. We didn't know it yet, but we were about to become ranchers.

28

LATE ONE EVENING, shortly before Christmas of 1966, Elvis rapped lightly on my door and called, "Sattnin, I have to talk to you." We had a password. Teasingly, I told him he'd have to utter it before I'd admit him. He laughed and said, "Fire Eyes"—the nickname I gave him when he was angry.

He had his old boyish grin on his face and his hands were behind his back. "Sit down, Sattnin, and close your eyes."

I did. When I opened my eyes, I found Elvis on his knees before me, holding a small black velvet box.

"Sattnin," he said.

I opened the box to find the most beautiful diamond ring I'd ever seen. It was three and a half karats, encircled by a row of smaller diamonds, which were detachable—I could wear them separately.

"We're going to be married," Elvis said. "You're going to be his. I told you I'd know when the time was right. Well, the time's right."

He slipped the ring on my finger. I was too overwhelmed to speak; it was the most beautiful and romantic moment of my life.

Our love would no longer be a secret. I'd be free to travel openly as Mrs. Elvis Presley without the fear of inspiring some scandalous headline. Best of all, the years of heartaches and fears of losing him to one of the many girls who were always auditioning for my role were over.

He was in a rush to show the ring to his father and Grandma and to tell them that we were officially engaged. I didn't even have a chance to get dressed. Considering our irregular life-style, getting engaged in my dressing room and showing off my beautiful diamond while dressed in a terrycloth robe didn't strike us as at all odd.

I wanted to share the great news with my parents, but he suggested we wait until we returned to L.A. a few weeks later. Then we could tell them in person; they deserved that consideration. That night, we called my parents and invited them to spend a weekend with us in Bel Air.

On the day they were due to arrive, Elvis was as excited as I'd ever seen him. He kept looking out the window, watching for their car. He was dying to show them the ring and almost did the moment they walked in the door, but I managed to keep my hand behind my back until we were all settled on the sofa. The second we were seated, he pulled my hand from behind me and said to my parents, "Well, we just wanted to show you this."

"What is it?" my father asked, peering at my hand.

"Well, sir, that's an engagement ring."

Tears trembled in my mother's eyes. "My God," she said softly. "It's beautiful."

They were both ecstatic. We loved letting them know that what they'd so long hoped and prayed for had now come to pass. We emphasized the importance of keeping our announcement a secret, asking them to maintain strict confidence even within the immediate family, since the kids might tell their friends at school and then word would be out. We wanted a private wedding, not a celebrity event. My parents agreed with all the plans. They couldn't have been happier, and all weekend they beamed with pleasure.

In the five years I'd lived with Elvis, I would rarely let them discuss marriage with Elvis. The possibility of their daughter being hurt was foremost in my parents' minds. Now they no longer had to worry whether they'd made the right decision in allowing me to leave home at such a young age.

I know that Colonel Parker asked him to take a long look at our relationship and decide where he wanted it to go. Elvis's attitude toward marriage was that it was *final*. Although he was monogamous by nature, he loved options. Still, he wasn't about to let me go. Curiously enough, after his talk with Colonel, it didn't take him long to decide the time was ripe.

It was his decision and his alone.

In our excitement we made the rest of our plans for the wedding ceremony. It was suggested I find a dress immediately, the reason being that if the news leaked out, we could get married at a moment's notice. But my search for a wedding dress ended up taking months. Disguised in dark glasses and a hat, I shopped every exclusive boutique from Memphis to L.A. where, despite my disguise, I was paranoid enough to think people recognized me. I even spoke with several seamstresses about designs but I didn't trust them enough to tell them it was for a wedding dress.

Finally someone suggested a little out-of-the-way shop in L.A. Charlie escorted me, posing as my fiancé, and it was here that I found my wedding dress. It wasn't extravagant, it wasn't extreme—it was simple and to me beautiful.

I glided out of the dressing room to model it for Charlie, and when he saw me, his eyes filled with tears. "You look beautiful, Beau," he said, and whispered, "He'll be so proud of you."

It was the February after our engagement. We were driving near Horn Lake, Mississippi, when we spotted a beautiful ranch—one hundred sixty acres of rolling hills. A herd of Santa Gertrudis cattle was grazing. There was a bridge across a little lake, a barn with stalls for horses, and a charming house situated in a prime location. It was for sale.

This was my perfect dream house. I fell in love with it and began to picture Elvis and me living there alone. It was small enough for me to handle myself. I could clean it and take care of Elvis, bringing him his breakfast in

Grandma Presley, always looking her best, 1967.

Presenting my brother Don with a new Mustang—it was quite a surprise.

Elvis with my sister Michelle and brothers Don, Tim, Jeff, and Tom.

Elvis relaxing in his room at Graceland.

The baby shower given by Nancy Sinatra. Ron Joy

Showing off Lisa Marie to proud grandparents—my father, left, Vernon, far right.

Elvis and me enjoying Lisa.

The good old days—Tom Jones and Elvis jamming.

Playing on the beach in Hawaii, 1968.

Hawaii.

Elvis's way of suntanning—with his electric fan—1969.

Colonel Parker playing with Lisa.

At the International Hotel in Las Vegas, 1969. UPI/Bettmann Newsphotos

Elvis navigating the boat—the Bahamas, 1969.

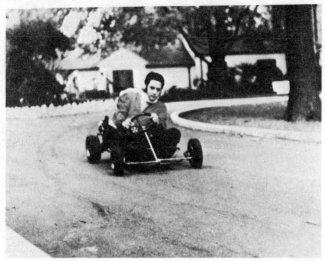

Elvis—one of his pastimes.

Me making sure everything is intact.

My mother preparing herself for the joyride.

Elvis cheating on
the Easter egg hunt
—he found his in
the refrigerator.

New Year's Eve, 1970.

My mother visiting Graceland.

Lisa on her way to Hawaii.

Elvis took this—one of his favorites.

Lisa deciding whether to take a little ride on my custom chopper.

Lisa relaxing with friends, Snoopy and Brutus.

Family picture.

Lisa and her daddy in Las Vegas on her birthday in 1973.

Vernon and Lisa, 1973.

Leaving Santa Monica Superior Court after the divorce, 1973. AP/
Wide World Photos

Four generations: (counterclockwise from top right) me, grandmother Lorana Iversen, my mother Ann Beaulieu, my sister Michelle Beaulieu Hovey, Lisa.

Lisa, Grandma, and Delta at Graceland.

Lisa and me clowning at Graceland.

Lisa.

Today. Lorimar

bed in the mornings as he gazed out at the gentle view of
Rising Sun grazing in the pastures.

I thought of this ranch as a wonderful way for us to
get away from Graceland from time to time. I pictured
us saddling our own horses and riding in the early
morning or at dusk. My picture was of us alone, without
an entourage.

We were determined to buy it, never foreseeing the
burden it would become. He wanted the ranch as much
as I did, even though Vernon said that at $500,000 it was
overpriced. He felt the owner could offer a much more
desirable deal and tried to persuade us that financially it
was not a good move. Elvis's movies were continuing to
decline in popularity and record sales were down. He
was averaging a million dollars a film and the money was
going out as quickly as it was coming in. Yet Elvis's
mind was made up. He wanted it.

Vernon grudgingly went to the bank to borrow
money, putting Graceland up as collateral. We bought
the entire ranch as was, including cattle and equipment,
and christened it the Circle G for Graceland.

We had eighteen horses by then, and all were transferred to the ranch as was the staff of nine. It was the
heyday of the commune, but Elvis had his own idea
about how he wanted us all to live. Since the house on
the property was small, he bought individualized mobile
homes and designated one to each family. Vernon
worked diligently to get permission from the city to put
gas and water on the ranch.

"Whatever it takes, do it," Elvis ordered.

Before long, tons of cement were being poured to

make the huge concrete foundations for the trailers. It didn't stop there. He bought El Caminos or Ranchero trucks for each family, even one for the plumber and another for the painter. He spent at least $100,000 on trucks alone.

He continued spending money as if it were going out of style. Alarmed, Vernon literally begged him to stop, but Elvis said, "I'm having fun, Daddy, for the first time in ages. I've got a hobby, something I look forward to gettin' up in the mornin' for."

It wasn't unusual to see him walking around the property, knocking on doors, waking everyone up, or checking on the horses in the early-morning hours. He was having a ball, and there were days he didn't even want to take time out to eat—he'd walk around with a loaf of bread under his arm in case hunger pangs struck. He loved shopping in Sears's basement, buying power tools, knives, flashlights, and other equipment that he would come bearing proudly back to the ranch.

That spring of 1967, we spent a lot of time there, sometimes staying as long as two weeks without returning to Graceland. On Sundays we had picnics and all the girls chipped in on potluck, bringing chicken baskets, cookies, and salads. We rode horses, held skeet-shooting contests, and combed the lake for turtles and snakes. There was fun, laughter, and a lot of camaraderie. Once again, our life was a group affair with everyone participating.

Even in my tiny house there'd be guests for dinner every night, usually single guys like Lamar and Charlie. Cooking for Elvis was easy: I'd just take whatever we were having and burn it. But there were so many others that his cousin Patsy would usually stop by to help me. The guys with wives would have dinner in their mobile homes and then come over for dessert and spend the rest of the evening with us.

There was always a lot of jamming. Elvis, Lamar Fike, and Charlie Hodge would get together in the middle of the room, harmonizing a favorite song. When they were really going good Elvis would yell, "Whew! Hot damn! One more time!" He'd sometimes spend an hour just on an ending because it had "the *feel*—the ingredients of a masterpiece."

Just as the entourage had followed us to the ranch, so did the curious. The same ones who gathered around Graceland started turning up at the Circle G and soon—day or night—scores of people were lined up along the fence. Since our little house stood in full view of the road, Elvis built a ten-foot-high wall, but nothing deterred them; now they began climbing on tops of cars and roofs of nearby homes. We couldn't get away from them, and I dreaded driving through the gates.

The dream was slowly turning into a nightmare. The wives wanted to get back to their homes, and the children wanted to get back to their friends and their schools.

Elvis liked it when everyone was together—on terms he alone specified—and he got upset when they wanted to leave. "Hell, I bought all this stuff," he said, "and everyone wants to go home." He resented defections; he'd given the employees everything and they didn't seem to appreciate it. He discovered that some of the regulars were selling their trucks. They needed the cash more than the El Caminos. Elvis couldn't imagine the financial struggle most people face and he never understood that the married regulars had to consider responsibilities to their wives and children.

Still, he enjoyed giving and sharing even as his own bank account was radically diminishing. An expensive hobby, the ranch had already cost him close to a million dollars and created a serious cash-flow problem. In daily phone calls to the Colonel, Vernon pleaded with him to come up with some work to divert Elvis from his spending spree. The Colonel promptly made arrangements for another movie, *Clambake*. Elvis read the script, yet another beach-and-bikini story, and hated it. Vernon convinced him he didn't have much choice. "We need the money, Son." And Elvis was committed.

"I don't wanna leave here, Cilla," he said. "I don't want to leave you, the ranch, Sun. Ain't no son of a bitch gonna keep me away long. That goes for Daddy, Colonel, the studios—no one. Their little plot to keep me from spending money ain't gonna work. If I need money, I'll go to Nashville and record a few songs. It'll be better than those lousy goddamn pictures."

Neither he nor Vernon ever considered turning the Circle G into a profit-making operation. All the necessities for a successful farm were present—tractors, feed, and the finest Santa Gertrudis cattle, bred on the Rockefeller ranch—but he sold the cattle after Vernon advised him that upkeep was too expensive. With professional financial counsel, Elvis might have pursued legitimate business ventures beneficial to him and his hobby.

Unfortunately, Vernon and Elvis were leery of business matters requiring financial advice. Vernon operated on pure instinct, refusing any suggestion of tax breaks, which he found too complicated to consider. He let the IRS figure Elvis's taxes and had done so ever since Elvis had been audited while in the Army and assessed eighty thousand dollars in back taxes. "Let's just pay the taxes, Daddy," Elvis said. "I make enough money. I'll make a million dollars and I'll give them half."

It was during the filming of *Clambake* that our lease on the house on Perugia Way in Los Angeles expired and we had to go looking for a new home. After our experience at the Circle G, we were concerned with protecting our privacy, and when we spotted a secluded home nestled against a hill in Bel Air, we thought we'd found sanctuary at last. But privacy was to elude us here as well.

Soon, hundreds of people began collecting on the mountain road directly above us and observing the view below through binoculars and telephoto lenses. We could no longer use our pool, patio, or driveway without looking up at an audience, including reporters and photographers who were having a field day trying to get candid photos and scoops.

The situation occasionally got out of hand. One night when Elvis went to Mount Washington to talk with Daya Mata and I was driving to Joan Esposito's for a visit, I noticed a car with bright headlights tailgating me. It was one of Elvis's most ardent fans, a two-hundred-pound female who was accompanied by another girl and a guy. Feeling unsafe, I decided to turn around and go home. She followed close all the way and by the time I drove through the gates, I was furious.

Seeing her drive up to the dead-end road above our house, I sped after her, parking my car broadside across the road, blocking her. She was standing beside her car when I strode up and demanded: "What are you doing here? Why are you following me?" She stood there mutely and again I demanded: "Why are you following me?"

"You whore," she snapped.

Incensed, I clenched my fist and swung an uppercut, hitting her in the face. She landed on the ground, spread-eagled and stunned. I landed on her and the two of us yelled, screamed, and pulled hair until I realized I needed help. I ran back to our front gate and yelled into the intercom, "Someone—Sonny, Jerry—come help me!"

Within seconds Elvis came flying out of the house with the guys close behind him. "What is it, Baby?"

When I explained, pointing to the ridge, Elvis went charging up the hill. Seeing him coming, the girl and her friends locked themselves in her car. Elvis was livid, lifting the car on its springs, bouncing it from side to side. He pounded the windshield, threatening to kill them if he ever got his hands on them or if they ever laid their hands on me.

"I'm underage! I'm underage!" she kept yelling. "I'll sue you if you touch me."

It took a lot of convincing from Sonny that she was more trouble than it was worth before Elvis would let her drive away.

29

ELVIS WAS SO despondent over *Clambake* that his weight ballooned from his usual 170 to 200 pounds by the time he reported for work. The studio ordered him to take the weight off—and fast. Enter the diet pills, the only way he could curb his appetite and reduce his weight in the short time allowed. Colonel managed to deal with the impatient studio brass.

The morning he was to begin shooting he awoke groggy and went into the bathroom while I was still in bed. I heard a loud thump, then cursing. "Goddamn motherfucking cord! Who the hell put this thing here?"

I jumped out of bed and ran into the bathroom, calling out, "What's happened?" He was lying on the floor, rubbing his head.

"I tripped over the goddamn TV cord. It was so

damned dark in here I didn't see it. Help me out of here—I have to lie down."

Although he was dizzy and off balance, we managed to make it to the bed. Feeling a big lump on his head, I called Joe Esposito at once, who summoned Colonel Parker and a doctor. Within minutes, the room was full of people—the doctor, his nurse, Colonel Parker, and several nervous studio executives. Colonel suggested that everyone but himself wait outside while the doctor made his diagnosis.

A few hours later it was announced that Elvis had a severe brain concussion and that the start of his film would be delayed indefinitely. The Colonel decided to use the accident to curtail some of Elvis's other activities. He wanted Elvis to abandon his involvement with esoteric philosophies, which the Colonel felt were irrelevant to Elvis's acting career and detrimental to clear thinking.

Elvis's spiritual quest hadn't gone unnoticed. Everyone from the entourage to film crews was aware of a change in his personality over the years he'd studied with Larry Geller. Elvis's vibrant personality was now passive and he was becoming more introverted. The mischievous games he'd once played on movie sets had been superseded by studious pursuits. Elvis buried his head in books that he diligently lugged to and from the studio every day.

The person most concerned about this change was Colonel Parker. The Colonel felt that Larry'd hypnotized Elvis, and his acting and recording careers were suffering as a result. Elvis's "concussion" provided an opportunity to put a halt to the soul-searching.

A few days after the accident, the Colonel gathered Elvis and the boys together for a meeting and told them they were burdening Elvis with too many problems. "Dealing with one person is one thing," he said, "but eleven, plus his own problems, is enough for any man to buckle under."

The Colonel told them that there were going to be some changes, from cutting back the payroll to taking problems to Joe Esposito instead of Elvis. His basic message was: Leave Elvis alone.

"Elvis should concentrate on his career," he said. "He's an artist, not a shoulder to cry on. Leave him alone, and let him do his work." The Colonel looked over at Larry; it was obvious that his message was primarily aimed at him. "I don't want him reading any more books and getting involved in things that clutter up his mind."

Elvis sat and listened like an obedient child, looking down, saying nothing. He did not stand up for Larry; no one did.

Later the Colonel told Elvis that he should get Larry out of his life, that Larry used some sort of technique to manipulate his thinking. Elvis argued that this wasn't the case. He was truly interested in his readings.

"You wouldn't be in this condition if your head was on straight," shouted the Colonel. "I'm telling you, Larry's jamming up your mind."

I was surprised at how attentively Elvis was listening. Elvis had always argued with anyone, even me, who said anything against Larry. At one point, it seemed Elvis would cut off his right arm for Larry. But now Elvis promised the Colonel he wouldn't spend any more time than he had to with him. He kept his promise. He only used Larry to style his hair and was never alone with him again.

After that meeting, the boys became openly hostile toward Larry, and even Elvis began making a few pointed remarks about him. Larry was now the outsider, and he eventually left. Colonel Parker was elated. His boy was back.

Elvis was ready for a major change and it was time to move on. The Colonel said his films were doing badly and he had to revitalize his career. He'd be getting married soon, and before that date he'd have to get his career and life back on track.

After Larry left, Elvis locked away many of his books. I told him I was glad, that they were literally destroying us. We were engaged to be married. "Would it make you feel better if I just got rid of them all?" Elvis asked. I nodded.

That night, at three in the morning Elvis and I piled a huge stack of his books and magazines into a large box and dumped them into an abandoned water well behind Graceland. We poured gasoline over the pile, lit a match, and kissed the past goodbye.

30

MY ATTITUDE TOWARD the usual wedding formalities was naive and unsophisticated. If it had not been for my good friend Joan Esposito, I can't imagine what I would have done. Joanie was great that way. She was raised in Missouri, where her mother was somewhat involved with political events and ventures. Joanie knew all the social graces along with proper etiquette.

Before the wedding there had never been an occasion for formalities—the same people came around for years and were always included when there was a special party such as New Year's at a local club or fireworks wars in back of Graceland.

She reminded me to order my own personalized stationery for later thank-yous and a guest book for later memories. She registered our name with the city's finest silver and crystal dealers for the convenience of family and friends buying wedding presents.

I had never attended a wedding as large as ours—nothing even close. I was nervous. The bounty from the wedding showers took me by surprise. Graceland had always seemed to have everything anyone could want. We were content with what was there, plus little things I'd bought over the years, such as simple dishes and plain glasses (in case of breakage).

"What's wrong with those?" I wondered. I was raised to be practical and it was showing. Joanie introduced me to dining luxury, the top names in silver, crystal, china—Baccarat, Lenox, Steuben.

The wedding ceremony itself took place on May 1, 1967. Colonel Parker handled the arrangements. His plan was for Elvis and me to drive from L.A. to our rented house in Palm Springs the day before the wedding, so that any inquisitive reporters who got wind of the event would think it was going to take place there.

In fact, we planned to rise before dawn on our wedding day and fly from Palm Springs to Las Vegas, where we were scheduled to arrive at the city clerk's office at 7 A.M. to get our marriage license. From there, the plan was to rush over to the Aladdin Hotel, dress, have a small ceremony in the private suite of the hotel's owner, and then—we hoped—slip out of town before anyone noticed.

Time was of the essence. We knew that once we applied for a marriage license, the news would flash around the world. It actually was only a few hours after we got our license that Rona Barrett's office began calling to ask if rumors about the marriage were true.

Elvis and I followed the Colonel's plan, but as we raced through the day we both thought that if we had it to do over again, we would have given ourselves more time. We were particularly upset at the way our friends and relatives ended up being shuffled around. The Colonel even told some of the boys that the room was too small to hold most of them and their wives, and that there wasn't time to change to a bigger room. Unfortunately, by the time Elvis found out, it was too late for him to do anything about it.

Now I sometimes look back at all the commotion of that week and wonder how things could have gotten so out of hand. I wish I'd had the strength then to say, "Wait a minute, this is *our* wedding, fans or no fans, press or no press. Let us invite whomever we want, and have it wherever we want!"

It seemed that as soon as the ceremony began, it was over. Our vows were taken. We were now husband and wife. I remember flashbulbs popping, my father's congratulations, my mother's tears of happiness.

I would have given anything for one moment alone with my husband. But we were immediately rushed out for a photo session, then a nationwide press conference, and finally a reception, with more photographers.

Mrs. Elvis Presley. It had a different ring, a nicer sound than previous labels such as "constant companion," "teen heartthrob," "live-in Lolita," "lover." For the first time, I felt accepted by my peers and the majority of the public. There were exceptions, of course—those who had that little hope that they might be the one to finally catch Elvis. I didn't understand that at the time. I was in love and just hoped they would be happy for us.

When I read in the newspapers that I was the best-kept secret in Hollywood, I felt very proud; it was good to be acknowledged. The years of doubt and insecurity of where and if I belonged were over.

I was both exhausted and relieved when we finally returned to Palm Springs aboard Frank Sinatra's Learjet, the *Christina*. There were more photographers and reporters waiting for us as we stepped off the plane, and others were parked outside our home.

I was surprised that Elvis was holding up so well, considering how nervous he'd been about this ultimate commitment. Yet he was charming with the press and dealt easily with endlessly clicking cameras and flashbulbs, all of which he could usually tolerate only for short periods of time. On top of everything else, we hadn't slept for nearly forty-eight hours.

In his own way, Elvis was determined that our wedding day would be special for us. He joked with Joe Esposito, asking, "Is this the way it's done?"

He carried me across the threshold of our house singing "The Hawaiian Wedding Song." He stopped and gave me a long, loving kiss, then proceeded to carry me up the stairs to our bedroom, the whole crowd teasing and applauding.

It was still daylight and the sun shone brightly through our bedroom windows as Elvis carefully placed me in the middle of our king-size bed.

I don't think he really knew what to do with me. After all, Elvis had protected me and saved me for so long. He was now understandably hesitant about fulfilling all his promises about how very good this moment was going to be.

Looking back, I have to laugh when I remember how nervous we both were. One would have thought that it was the first time we had ever been together under intimate circumstances.

Gently, his lips touched mine. Then he looked deeply into my eyes. "My wife," he said softly, as he drew me close. "I love you, Cilla," he murmured, covering my body with his.

The intensity of emotion I was experiencing was electrifying. The desire and lust that had built up in me throughout the years exploded in a frenzy of passion.

Could he have known how it would be for me? Had he planned this all along? I'll never know. But I do know that as I went from child to woman, the long, romantic, yet frustrating adventure that Elvis and I had shared all seemed worthwhile. As old-fashioned as it might sound, we were now one. It was special. *He* made it special, like he did with anything he took pride in.

31

WITHIN A FEW DAYS we were in Memphis, where Dee Presley held a small wedding shower for me. At the end of May we threw a big reception at Graceland for all *our* friends and relatives—and some fans. Elvis and I wore our wedding clothes, greeted everyone, sipped champagne, and shared cake just as if the party were taking place after the wedding ceremony. It was much more comfortable and relaxed than Las Vegas.

Laughing and somewhat high from the champagne, we could really have a good time. There were no photographers or strangers watching our every move.

It was fun seeing Vernon get loose.

"Daddy, you want some more champagne?" Elvis asked, his eyes twinkling.

"Don't mind if I do, Son. That's pretty good stuff."

"Yeah. Well, don't drink too much. I don't want my daddy gettin' in trouble. I see that blonde you've been eyein'."

Vernon stole a glance at the girl and, with the same twinkle replied, "She ain't too bad, is she? Think I'll go see if she needs anything."

Elvis turned to me and said, "I like seein' Daddy happy. He hasn't had too much of it lately, poor ol' guy." He watched Vernon make his way through the crowd.

The reception at Graceland was our way of trying to make everyone happy—those who hadn't known about the wedding ceremony, those who knew but couldn't attend, and those who knew but weren't invited. It was a way of including everyone, of making up to anyone whose feelings might have been hurt during the rushed hours in Vegas.

One person who had been very upset was Red West. He had not been invited to the wedding ceremony in the suite, only to the reception afterward. I believe the reason Red was so hurt was because Elvis did not demand that he be present, did not take a stand over Colonel Parker's decision that only the immediate family and best man attend. I also believe that Red wanted to be best man. After all, he'd known Elvis the longest, since their days at Humes High. When Red found out he could not watch the ceremony, he refused to come at all.

Elvis was aware of Red's decision but was determined not to let anything mar the wedding. I understood that but was never able to figure out how Marty Lacker made it to the ceremony. In a last-minute decision Elvis had included him as best man along with Joe Esposito.

It took a long time for Red to come around again without showing his displeasure. This bothered Elvis and he discussed it with many of us, justifying himself and blaming Colonel for putting him in an awkward position.

"You didn't make the decision—I did," Colonel reportedly stated. "No matter who you picked, there was gonna be someone left mad. You got too many as it is. You oughta listen to me and let go of some of 'em, then these things won't come up."

There's an old Southern belief that holds that a woman goes into a marriage thinking she can change her man, while a man wants his woman to stay the same as when he married her. I didn't want to change Elvis, but I did have the romantic delusion that once we were married, I could change our life-style.

For the first few days after the wedding, I thought my dream had come true. We divided our time between Graceland and the ranch, where Elvis and I had taken up residence in a large, three-bedroom trailer.

It was typical of Elvis to choose the trailer over the quaint little house. He had never lived in a trailer before and it intrigued him. The place was completely furnished, including a washer, a dryer, and a modern kitchen. It turned out to be very romantic.

I loved playing house. I personally washed all his clothes, along with the towels and sheets, and took pride in ironing his shirts and rolling up his socks the way my mother had taught me. Here was an opportunity to take care of him myself. No maids or housekeepers to pamper us. No large rooms to embrace the regular entourage.

I got up early, put on a pot of coffee, and started his breakfast with a pound of bacon and three eggs, proudly presented it to him the moment he woke up.

"You see, if we were ever stranded somewhere alone, you know I can take care of you."

It must have been difficult for him to eat the instant he opened his eyes—but he wasn't going to disappoint his new bride.

Although the rest of the group traveled with us, they respected our privacy as newlyweds and, for the most part, left us alone.

I understood Elvis's need for the camaraderie the entourage provided, and I didn't want to take him away from the people he loved, especially now that we were married. He had always criticized wives who tried to change the status quo. He told me about one wife, saying, "She doesn't like him to be around the boys so much. She's going to cause problems in the group." The last thing I wanted was for Elvis to think I'd be the kind of wife who'd come between her man and his friends.

I decided one evening to show off my cooking skills for everyone by making one of Elvis's favorite dishes, lasagna. I invited the regulars, bragging to one and all about how well I prepared this Italian specialty. Despite my outward confidence, I must have made ten long-distance calls to my mother in New Jersey, checking and rechecking on quantities and measurements. It was important for me to prove myself a success. Joe Esposito, our only Italian and a "gourmet chef," kidded me all week about how he bet that my lasagna wouldn't be as good as his. All that ribbing only made me more nervous. I kept thinking, What do I know about pasta? I'm not even Italian.

Finally, the night of the dinner came. Everyone was seated at the table, watching me expectantly. I tried to appear cool and confident as I brought out the fancily prepared platter and started cutting individual squares for my guests. I did notice that when I started slicing the lasagna, it felt a little tough, but thinking I was holding a dull knife, I continued dishing it out.

I sat down, smiled anxiously, and said, "Please start." We all took a bite and—crunch. There was a look of shock on everyone's face. I looked at my plate and was mortified when I realized I had forgotten to boil the pasta.

Elvis began laughing, but when he saw I was about to cry he turned to his plate and began eating, uncooked noodles and all. Taking their lead from him, everyone followed suit.

Joe Esposito still laughs about it, frequently saying, "Cilla? How about some lasagna?"

32

ELVIS AND I often talked of having children, but we certainly weren't planning on having them right away. Then one day we were at the ranch. It was early afternoon and Elvis was still asleep. I lay in bed and felt a strange sensation in my stomach, a sensation I'd never felt before. I lay staring at the ceiling. No—it couldn't be. Again, the same feeling. I slid out of bed. I'll call Patsy, I thought. She'd know. I went to the phone in the next room.

"Patsy, when you found out you were pregnant, did you feel strange?"

"Strange like what?"

"You know. I mean, what did you feel?"

"Well, I missed my period."

"But didn't you feel something in your body, something strange?"

"I really don't remember, Priscilla. Why?"

"Because I think I'm pregnant. I know I am. I've never felt this before."

"Maybe it's nerves."

"No—I just have a funny feeling. I'll talk to you later."

I didn't tell Elvis right away: I couldn't. But he saw that I was quiet and preoccupied.

If I were pregnant, I knew that our plans to travel would have to be postponed. I wouldn't be able to head off to some exotic locale and leave my child with nurses and maids. For the first year, I truly wanted to be alone with Elvis, without any responsibilities or obligations.

For a few days I was angry with Elvis. Before the wedding I asked him if I should start taking birth-control pills, but he had been adamantly against it.

"They're not good for you. I really don't want you taking them. They're not perfected yet, Baby. There's all kinds of side effects."

A week passed before I told Elvis my suspicions. I expected him to react with the same mixed emotions I'd felt, but he was ecstatic. He made arrangements for me to see a doctor right away, accompanied me to the doctor's office, and sat anxiously in the waiting room while I was examined.

When I came out I put my arms around him and said, "Guess what?"

"What? What?" He was barely able to contain himself.

"You're going to be a daddy."

He couldn't believe it and immediately wanted to tell everyone. Just then his father, who had driven over with us, came into the room. Elvis grabbed him.

"Daddy, you won't believe this. Cilla's gonna have a baby. You're gonna be a granddaddy."

"Good Lord Almighty," Vernon said, stunned. "You're kiddin' me."

"No, Daddy. We're telling you the truth." Then Elvis teased him, saying, "You're going to be a gray-headed granddaddy."

I loved seeing Elvis happy, but I was still uncertain about how my unexpected pregnancy would affect our marriage. This was supposed to have been our time alone. I wanted to be beautiful for him; instead, my debut as Elvis's bride was going to be spoiled by a fat stomach, puffy face, and swollen feet.

As far as I was concerned, the less people mentioned about my looking pregnant, the better. I intended to prove that a pregnant woman did not have to get fat. I wanted to refute Elvis's claim that "women use the excuse of their pregnancy to let themselves go." Although the doctor said that a twenty-five-pound gain would be fine, I immediately dropped from my normal one hundred ten pounds to one hundred. During the next four months, I regained just five pounds, and only nine more by the time of delivery. Eating one meal a day and snacking on apples and hard-boiled eggs, I prided myself on never needing to buy a maternity outfit. My doctor advised that in addition to taking multiple vitamins I should consume plenty of dairy products. Being vain, I amended my doctor's instructions and lessened my intake of dairy products. I did not want to gain weight and get stretch marks. As a further precaution I resolved to slather myself with cocoa butter for the next eight months.

A few days after I learned I was pregnant, we left Memphis for L.A., where Elvis was to begin preproduction on a new film, *Speedway*. It was to be the last drive in our customized bus before it was sold. During the trip, Elvis and the guys had a ball, punching each other and playing practical jokes. I played photographer, clicking away at everyone. But when I kept smiling and laughing I still felt very ambivalent about my pregnancy. I wanted a baby, just not so soon.

Elvis was extremely sensitive to my moods. He missed his little girl's "twinkling eyes," her "bright, smiling face." Finally, in Flagstaff, Arizona, at a small roadside inn, he sat me down and said, "What do you want to do, Little One?"

I broke down and answered, "I don't know. What can I do?"

"What do you think?" he said. "I'll back you up whatever you want to do."

Instantly I knew what he was talking about. He was leaving the decision up to me. "It's our baby," I said, sobbing. "I could never live with myself, neither could you."

There were no words, only his smile of approval; he held me tightly in his arms as I cried. The two of us, bound by love, accepted our new little creation wholeheartedly.

33

WHEN I FIRST felt my baby move I suddenly understood the full joy of carrying our child. My smile returned when Elvis delicately placed his hand on my slightly swollen stomach and said, "How can such a little creature carry another little young'un?" The pregnancy was bringing us closer. He would call me from the studio every day, just to say hello and make sure I was fine. It was because of the baby that we decided to buy our first home in Los Angeles instead of leasing as we'd done in the past. While he was filming I searched the Beverly Hills–Bel Air area for a place that would suit us.

Later that fall, when we were in Arizona for location filming on *Stay Away, Joe*, I saw an advertisement in *Variety* for a house that sounded perfect: a beautiful home in Trousdale Estates, completely furnished, three bedrooms, a guest cottage, pool, and good security.

I flew back to L.A. The house was owned by a prominent landowner who was recently divorced. With a built-in bar, antique furnishings, and collectors' art, it was a far cry from Rocca Place, where each room was decorated to each employee's specification—a different carpet, a different color, a different style in each room. Unfortunately, I'd tried to satisfy everyone's taste, and architectural indigestion was the result. This time I would be able to live with everything the way I liked.

As soon as Elvis returned from Arizona we moved into our new home and began preparing a room for our baby. All I could think about was how happy I was, how wonderful life was.

Naturally, I got a lot of advice about what I should and shouldn't do while I was pregnant. Steeped in her Southern superstitions, Grandma was especially solicitous, telling me I couldn't brush my hair over my head or else I would wrap the umbilical cord around the baby. She also said I shouldn't stand on my feet too long or my legs would swell and I wouldn't be able to walk again. She was as concerned as any doting mother and some of my activities gave her reason to worry. I still kept up with my ballet, rode my motorcycle and my horse Domino, right up until the eighth month of pregnancy. Elvis thought I was absolutely incredible to keep up with him in every way. That made me happy. I was pleasing him and still by his side every day.

Then I began hearing rumors about Elvis and Nancy Sinatra, the same rumors that I had read about in Germany: that she had a passionate crush on him, that they were having an affair. I was extremely sensitive and quick to cry. Elvis assured me that I was just being over-sensitive because of my condition. I agreed. Six months into my pregnancy Nancy called and said she'd like to give me a baby shower. I didn't know her that well and thought it a little strange that she was so accommodating. But Elvis assured me that she was very nice and that I should get to know her. It was agreed that I would go to the shower under one condition, which Colonel suggested: All the pictures that were taken that day were to be handed over to me. That way, there'd be no shots popping up in the national movie magazines. It turned out quite nicely. Nancy was very friendly and very supportive. I found that I liked her and I decided to ignore the rumors.

Life takes such surprising turns. Just when you're getting confident, along comes the unexpected. I was upstairs at Graceland when Elvis called me to his office, the one adjoining my dressing room. "Cilla, I have to have time to think. Things just aren't going right. It'll be good for the two of us to take a little time off, like a trial separation. Be apart from one another for a while."

I wanted to die. I was seven months along and could not believe what I was hearing. It had to be a joke. "What are you saying? What did I do?"

"You didn't do anything, Baby. You don't understand. It's not you. It's just that I'm going through some things. I think it'd be better if we took a little break."

I looked at him in silence, feeling a new strength. If he excluded me at this time, then he didn't deserve me at all. I stood up and said, "You've got it. Just tell me when to leave." I went into my dressing room and closed the door.

I was numb. This was not the man I knew. I instinctively withdrew, my affection numbed, my thoughts suspicious, my heart aching.

I don't think Elvis really intended to leave me. It wasn't his style. I later realized he too had questions about how a baby would affect his life. Would his public accept him as a father? He wasn't even sure if his fans had adapted to his becoming a husband. How loyal would they be?

Within a short time Elvis's sensitive nature brought him back to his senses. Two days had passed. The idea of a trial separation was never mentioned again. We both acted as if nothing had been said. It was at times like this that I wished Elvis and I had the ability to truly communicate with each other, to confront our insecurities, fears, and frustrations instead of pretending these feelings weren't there. We probably would have been surprised at how much understanding we both really had. I could not escape the impact his words had on me, leaving me with a sense of doubt.

As my pregnancy progressed, we still played hard. I wanted to be included in everything that everyone else did. That Christmas we went to the ranch and rode horses, had snowball fights and went on hayrides. Elvis would sit up front in the wagon and call out to me, "How you doing, Cilla? That's my girl. How's she doing back there?"

I'd call back, "She's doing pretty good. I'm okay."

If we'd go horseback riding, he'd always ask me, "Are

you sure you can do this? Did the doctor say you could?"

"Yes," I'd answer. "I can do it."

I was determined not to ask for special treatment.

It was only in the last month or so that I slowed down at all. Instead of sitting through two or three films a night, Elvis would take me home after just one.

He arranged his schedule so that he could be home with me at Graceland during the final month. To be absolutely prepared for the big day, we even performed practice drills for the trip to Baptist Memorial Hospital. As my time drew near, Elvis became more and more nervous.

On February 1, 1968, I awoke about eight o'clock and found the bed beneath me soaking wet. Frightened, I called my mother in New Jersey and she suggested I ring the doctor immediately. He told me to head straight for the hospital. I gently woke Elvis up and told him the big day had arrived. Elvis groggily asked me if I was sure. When I said yes, he called Vernon and told him to notify everyone, then yelled downstairs, "She's ready! Cilla's going to have the baby!"

Ignoring his frenzy, I disappeared calmly into the bathroom and applied my ever-so-black mascara and teased my ever-so-black hair. Later at the hospital I requested special permission to keep on my double set of lashes.

Downstairs there was pandemonium. As planned, the decoy cars raced off first, Lamar and Joe frantically waving for the fans to follow them. Then we took off, but despite the rehearsals we headed straight for the wrong hospital. We had changed hospitals, but obviously Jerry, who was driving, hadn't been informed. Charlie Hodge saved the day, convincing Jerry it was Baptist Memorial, not Methodist. Luckily we arrived in time.

Our daughter, Lisa Marie, was born at 5:01 that afternoon. The nurse brought her into my room and I cradled her in my arms. I couldn't believe she was mine, that I had borne this child. She was so tiny, so beautiful. Elvis came into the room and kissed me, thrilled that we had a perfectly normal, healthy baby. He was already in love with her. He watched me holding her and his eyes misted with happiness. Then he took us both in his arms and held us.

"Nungen," he whispered, which was his way of saying "young one." "Us has a little baby girl."

"Her knows," I whispered back.

I asked if he wanted to hold her. He looked petrified at first, but then he started to touch her. He played with her hands, her feet. He was in awe, saying, "I can't believe that I made part of this beautiful child." Elvis knew that I had wanted the baby to have dark hair like his, and Lisa had been born with lots of silky black hair. "She's so perfect," he said, "even the color of her hair is right."

We stayed in each other's arms for a long time, caressing our infant and each other, a young couple sharing the first pleasures of parenthood.

The man in my hospital room that day was the man I loved, and will always love. He didn't have to try to be strong and decisive or sexy, he wasn't afraid to show his warmth or vulnerability. He didn't have to act the part of Elvis Presley, superstar. He was just a man, my husband.

34

IN MY DIARY entry dated April 5, I wrote, "The baby's getting more beautiful as each day goes by. Dr. Turman said she's healthy and progressing well. Elvis went with me to the pediatrician, waiting outside in the car. He also accompanied me to the obstetrician. He's insisting I keep up with my regular checkups—taking care of both of us like a doting father.

"But I've been lonely for him since the baby's birth; he is still withdrawn. It's been two months and he still hasn't touched me. I'm getting concerned."

The following day, I wrote, "I asked Elvis if anything was wrong, if he's lost his desire for me. I saw this made him a little uncomfortable. He told me he wants to make sure my system's back to normal—that he doesn't want to hurt me. That made me feel a little better.

"We brought Lisa to our room, put her in the middle of the bed with us. She's such a good baby—we can't believe she's ours."

Elvis and I started getting back into our regular routine. Since the baby was born, we were spending more time at Graceland, eventually moving all the horses back to the original stables, Vernon selling much of the equipment and, later, the Circle G itself.

Elvis accepted fatherhood with a great deal of joy, but the fact that I was a mother had a disquieting effect on him. I didn't understand at the time, but later on I would learn more about men who are very close to their own mothers. I am no purveyor of Freudian theory. I believe when a man comes into the world, his first unconditional love is his mother. She cuddles him, gives him warmth, the breast for nourishment, and everything he needs to exist. None of those feelings has a sexual connotation. Later, when his own wife becomes a mother, this bank of memories is ripped open and his passion may dissipate.

When Elvis's mother was alive they had been unusually close. Elvis even told her about his amatory adventures, and many nights when she was ill, he would sleep with her. All the girls he took out seriously had to fulfill Gladys's requirements of the ideal woman. And as with me, Elvis then put the girl on a pedestal, "saving her" until the time was sacred and right. He had his wild times, his flings, but any girl he came home to he had to respect.

Now I was a mother and he was uncertain how to treat me. He had mentioned before we were married that he had never been able to make love to a woman who'd had a child. But throughout my pregnancy—until the last six weeks—we had made love passionately. He'd been very careful each time, afraid that he might hurt the baby or me, but he was always loving and sensitive to my needs. Now months had passed.

On April 20 I wrote in my diary: "I embarrassed myself last night. I wore a black negligee, laid as close to Elvis as I could while he read. I guess it was because I knew what I wanted and was making it obvious. I kissed his hand, then each finger, then his neck and face. But I waited too long. His sleeping pills had taken effect. Another lonely night."

Finally, months later Elvis made love to me. Before we made love, he told me I was a young mother now, that being the mother of his child is very special. But I wrote in my diary, "I am beginning to doubt my own sexuality as a woman. My physical and emotional needs were unfulfilled."

35

We returned to Los Angeles, where Elvis was filming *Live a Little, Love a Little*. He started getting into his old habits again. Frustrated, I started searching for dance classes to enroll in. I looked through the local Yellow Pages until one class caught my attention, a school for jazz and ballet not far from home.

The studio was small and unpretentious; the owner, Mark, was an extremely attractive and dynamic man of forty-five. He was an excellent dancer and a fine teacher, and by the time I left that afternoon, I had enrolled for private lessons.

Still too shy to dance in front of a group, I wanted to wait until I was sure I could keep up with the other dancers before taking a class. I began taking private lessons three times a week. Mark's personal interest and attention were flattering, and I was soon doing lifts and jumps, things I'd never thought I could accomplish.

He said I had the potential to be a good dancer, and he pushed me to the limit. Out of frustration and pain I would want to quit. Demanding that I continue, he told me I was building character and forced me to repeat the same routine until it was nearly perfected. This made me realize that I could go further than I'd ever dreamed.

He believed in me, and I was accomplishing something. For the first time I was creating, feeling good about myself, and I couldn't wait to get to class each day.

Mark was charismatic and I was particularly vulnerable. In lieu of a passionate marriage, dance was becoming my life; I was obsessed with it, taking all my frustrations and feelings into the studio. I found myself thinking about Mark even when I was home. I had only seen him a few times in my life and yet I was unable to get him out of my mind. I rationalized, telling myself it was because he was always *there* for me. He seemed to understand me, while the man I truly loved was involved in his own world. I began to relax, enjoying myself almost against my will. It had been a while since I'd spent some time with a man who validated my abilities and appreciated spending time with me alone. It was also the first time I was not competing for my own identity. This was a high I had not experienced recently. I had a brief affair and decided to end it.

I came out of it realizing I needed much more out of my relationship with Elvis. Elvis and I decided to get away to Hawaii.

This was the first time we'd gone on holiday, and I

was hoping that it would be a second honeymoon, that my experience with Mark would be forgotten. We took along Lisa, her nurse, Joe, Joanie, Patsy and her husband, Gee Gee, Lamar and his wife Nora, and Charlie. We checked into the Ilikai Hotel on Waikiki, but soon found that Elvis couldn't go to the beach without attracting a crowd. We decided to rent a house on a private beach and spent the rest of our vacation there.

We had a great time, and Elvis and I were like two kids again, away from the pressures and the filming—and away from Mark, to whom my attention would occasionally wander.

It was there that we met Tom Jones, and Elvis became very fond of him. He had always enjoyed Tom's vocal style, especially in "Green, Green Grass of Home," which Elvis had first heard while traveling from L.A. to Memphis. He'd called me when they'd stopped in Arizona, encouraging me to get the record.

Elvis was positive Tom was black; no white singers could belt out a song like that, except the Righteous Brothers, who much to his surprise were also white.

Tom Jones and Elvis enjoyed an instant rapport. After an appearance at the Ilikai, Tom invited us to his suite, along with our group. Within minutes the champagne exploded and the party was on. We laughed, drank, joked, drank some more (lots more), jammed—and reeled back to the Ilikai at dawn. Elvis had had such a good time he personally invited Tom and his group to join us the next day at our beach house. A friendship was born, a friendship of mutual respect and admiration.

One of Elvis's outstanding attributes was his conviction that there was room for anyone with talent in the entertainment field. In my experience, only a few stars are this generous. Greed, insecurity, jealousy, ego usually keep celebrities from supporting one another.

Elvis could spot talent instantly. In Las Vegas, we regularly took in lounge acts featuring various up-and-coming artists, and if Elvis liked the show, he patronized the club, encouraging the entertainers to pursue their careers, infusing them with confidence and enthusiasm.

Some of his favorites were Ike and Tina Turner, Gary Puckett and the Union Gap, dancers Tybe and Bracia, and old-timers Fats Domino and the Ink Spots, all talented people deserving acknowledgment in their craft.

One night we visited Barbra Streisand backstage at the International Hotel, now the Hilton. It was a classic Streisand performance and Elvis, after a few too many Bloody Marys, wanted to tell Barbra his impressions. We were ushered backstage to her dressing room and Elvis's first words upon meeting her were: "What did you ever see in Elliott Gould? I never could stand him."

In typical Streisandese she retorted, "Whaddya mean? He's the fah-tha of my child!"—leaving Elvis speechless.

Elvis had some other very special favorites—Arthur Prysock, John Gary, opera star Robert Merrill, Brook Benton, Roy Orbison, and Charles Boyer's recording "Where Has Love Gone?"

He couldn't abide singers who were, in his words, "all technique and no emotional feeling" and in this category he firmly placed Mel Torme and Robert Goulet. They were both responsible for two television sets being blown away with a .357 Magnum.

36

ELVIS'S FIVE-YEAR contract with MGM was up in 1968 and he was finally free to move on to new challenges. Even Colonel admitted that Elvis's career needed a shot in the arm. NBC made him an offer to do his own television special, with newcomer Steve Binder directing. There was no initial format, but the idea was tempting and the money was right. The fact that there was no script—that it was an "open development"—made Colonel hesitant to agree. Colonel demanded more control than that, but Elvis wanted to meet Steve, make sure that they could get along, speak the same language.

It had been years since Elvis had appeared on TV and he was nervous. To his surprise, Steve was much younger than he had anticipated, extremely perceptive, and soft-spoken, a startling contrast to the studio heads he'd worked with, men much older, with hardened, preconceived opinions on how Elvis should be packaged and sold. For the first time in years he felt creative. Steve Binder gained Elvis's trust and had the sensitivity to let Elvis just be Elvis. Steve observed, took mental notes, learned Elvis's ways, discovered what made his star comfortable and what got him uptight.

During their meetings Steve sensed Elvis's fear that he hadn't been before a live audience in years but he noticed that Elvis came alive backstage in the dressing room jamming with the musicians.

Each day he grew more confident and excited about his new project, taking pride once again in his appearance, watching his weight, following his diet, and working closely with the show's costume designer, Bill Belew, creating a look we hadn't seen him sport in years—the black leather suit.

I was surprised when he said, "Sattnin, I feel a little silly in that outfit. You think it's okay?"

Elvis knew this special was a big step in his career. He could not fail. For two straight months he worked harder than on all his movies combined. It was the most important event in his life.

During this time I was discovering whole new worlds of music—Segovia; Blood, Sweat and Tears; Tchaikovsky; Santana; Mason Williams; Ravel; Sergio

Mendes; Herb Alpert—and I was anxious to share my new enthusiasms, music and dance, with my husband. I wanted to bring energy to our relationship in the hope of strengthening our marriage. Discussions at the dinner table now included Leonard Bernstein and Carlos Montoya, but they held no appeal for Elvis; the TV special was consuming all his thoughts.

He was away much of the time, and when we did see each other our level of communication was strictly superficial. Each absorbed in our own separate pursuits, we had little in common except our daughter. My approach with him was delicate: I was aware of the distance growing between us. But because of his preoccupation with the special, I realized that the last thing he needed from me was a statement that I feared we were drifting apart.

In his absence, I was taking care of Lisa in addition to attending dance classes in the morning, ballet in the early evening, and two jazz classes at night, lasting often until one in the morning. I was now studying with a new dance instructor, who was using me to give demonstrations for the evening classes. Many of the students were professional dancers. I had diligently worked my way into the company, rehearsing four hours every day to master new steps, constantly pushing myself to new limits, and eventually I was to take a place in the dance company, anonymously performing shows on weekends at colleges in the L.A. area.

Elvis's Singer TV special was a huge success, the highest-rated special of the year, and his finale, "If I Can Dream," was his first million-selling record in years. We sat around the TV watching the show, nervously anticipating the response. Elvis was quiet and tense through the whole program, but as soon as the calls started, we all knew he had a new triumph. He hadn't lost his touch. He was still the King of Rock and Roll.

It was a blessing for both of us. The hours I devoted to dance released him from the strain of my dependence. My new interest didn't pose a threat in the sense that taking up a profession would have. I was still there to tend to his needs, as he wanted his wife to be, while also creating my own world, no longer intimidated by the magnitude of his. I was growing, learning, and expanding as an individual.

This new freedom nearly came to an abrupt end when a newcomer to the clan decided to take it upon himself to investigate my comings and goings. He reported to Elvis that I was seen coming out of a dance studio at a late hour and did Elvis want him to carry it any further. Elvis's unpredictability in dealing with certain crises in life could be astounding. Logically, such a volatile man would explode. Instead, he made no accusations. His only comment was, "Little One, there are some people who are insinuating you've been seen coming out of a dance studio at late hours."

"It's true. You know I'm part of the company. It's not just me leaving. That's the time we break."

I pleaded with him to tell me who was starting trouble. All he would say was, "Let's put it this way: He's new and he's treading on dangerous ground. If he knows what's good for him, he better keep the fuck to his own business."

After the success of his special, Elvis devoted several weeks to a recording session, and again he was highly motivated. For the first time in fourteen years, he'd been persuaded to record in Memphis, at the American Sound Studios, a black company where major artists, including Aretha Franklin, had recorded their most recent hits. The studio musicians were young and Elvis had a great rapport with them. More importantly, he made great music with them.

He'd be at the studio singing until the early-morning hours and then return the next evening, full of energy and ready to start again. His voice was in top form and his excitement was infectious. Each cut was more terrific than the one before. We'd listen to the songs over and over, Elvis yelling, "All right, listen to that sound," or "Goddamn, play it again."

Colonel stayed away from this session. Elvis was the artist, and he was on a roll. He ended up recording so many songs, it took RCA a year and a half to release them all, including hits like "In the Ghetto," "Kentucky Rain," and "Suspicious Minds."

Watching Elvis sing with confidence again, honing each word in his own style, filled us all with pride. What a contrast to sessions in the past that had been filled with anger, frustration, and disappointment, resulting in late arrivals or, on occasion, no-shows.

At one point he looked over at me, smiled, then casually started singing "From a Jack to a King." He knew it was a favorite of mine. Later he sang "Do You Know Who I Am?" As I listened to the words, I couldn't help but relate to them.

After four years of lackluster songs, he was back on the charts again, and RCA could no longer complain about him. They'd been threatening the Colonel that if Elvis didn't have a recording session soon, they were going to rerelease some of his old songs.

One success led to another. Since his TV special, he was eager to begin performing in front of a live audience again, to prove to everyone that he hadn't lost his touch. Looking for the best source of immediate income, the Colonel made a deal with the nearly completed Las Vegas International for Elvis to headline there for a month, at a salary of half a million dollars.

Vegas was the challenge he needed to demonstrate that he could still captivate a live audience. This was what he loved most and did best. But it was a major challenge.

He hadn't made any real demands on his voice in years and now was locked into two shows a night for twenty-eight days straight. Anxious, he wondered whether he was up to the strain, whether he'd draw sell-out crowds, whether he would be able to hold an audience for a full two hours. He wanted this new act to be accepted, feeling he now had more than his rock-and-roll gyrations to offer.

Not only was this a crucial time in his career, but there was the additional pressure of the unprecedented fee and the fact that Las Vegas was the only city where he'd bombed, thirteen years earlier, in 1956.

He wasn't the kind of person who'd come out and say, "I'm scared." Instead I'd see it in his actions, his left leg shaking, and his foot tapping. He held in his fears and emotions until at times he would explode, tearing into anyone who happened to be around. At dinner one evening Elvis said that he was concerned about his hairstyle, and I mentioned I'd seen a billboard of Ricky Nelson on Sunset Boulevard. His hair was long with a slight wave, and I thought it was extremely appealing. I innocently suggested that Elvis take a look at it. "Are you goddamn crazy?" he shouted. "After all these years, Ricky Nelson, Fabian, that whole group have more or less followed in my footsteps, and now I'm supposed to copy them? You've gotta be out of your mind, woman."

He left the dinner table in a rage. He had always been hailed as an original and now he was afraid that in Vegas even that wouldn't be enough. I knew I had injured his ego and for that I apologized.

In preparing his show for the International, Elvis pulled out all the stops. He was in top form—on a natural high quite independent of pills. He was more trim and physically fit than he'd ever been.

Putting together the best musicians, sound and lighting technicians, costumers, and choreographers, he was taking no chances this time. He scoured the music scene for the top sidemen in the business. Auditions were held and he handpicked each player—names such as James

Burton, John Wilkinson, Ronny Tutt, Glen D. Hardin, Jerry Scheff. He loved the sound of the Sweet Inspirations, backup group for Aretha Franklin, and he hired them on the spot as a warmup act and to sing backup vocals. He also hired his favorite gospel group, the Imperial Quartet.

Before leaving Los Angeles, Elvis rehearsed at RCA Sound Studios for ten days and then polished the act for a full week prior to the opening. It was the event of the summer in Vegas. Colonel Parker brought the preopening publicity to fever pitch. Billboards were up all over town. On the third floor of the International, administrative offices bustled with activity. No other entertainer coming into Vegas had ever stimulated this kind of excitement. The hotel lobby was dominated by Elvis paraphernalia—pictures, posters, T-shirts, stuffed animals, balloons, records, souvenir programs. You'd think Barnum and Bailey were coming to town.

Back home there was also excitement as we girls discussed what we'd wear to the opening. "I want you to look extra special, Baby," Elvis said. "This is a big night for all of us." I hit every boutique in West L.A. before finding just the right outfit.

Though it had been nine years since Elvis had given a live performance, you never would have known it from his opening. The audience cheered the moment he stepped onstage and never stopped the entire two hours as Elvis sang, "All Shook Up," "Blue Suede Shoes," "In the Ghetto," "Tiger Man," and "Can't Help Falling in Love." He mixed the old with the new, the fast and hot with the lyrical and romantic. It was the first time I'd ever seen Elvis perform live. Wanting to surprise me, he had kept me from rehearsals. I was astounded. At the end he left them still cheering and begging for more.

Cary Grant was among the stars who came backstage to congratulate him after the show. But the most touching moment was when Colonel Parker arrived with tears in his eyes, wanting to know where his boy was. Elvis came out of the dressing room and the two men embraced. I believe everyone felt their emotion in that moment of triumph.

I don't think we slept that night. Joe Esposito brought in all the newspapers and we read the rave reviews declaring, "Elvis was great" and "He never looked or sang better." He shared credit for his new success with all of us.

"Well, we did it. It's going to be a long thirty days, but it's going to be worth it if we get the reception we got last night. I may have been a real tyrant, but it was well worth it."

"Yeah, you're right," we all agreed, laughing. "You were a tyrant."

The International Hotel was delirious over Elvis's performance and the box-office receipts. The following day they signed a five-year contract with the Colonel for Elvis to appear twice a year, usually around the same time, January and August, at the then unheard-of salary of one million dollars a year.

Elvis literally took over Las Vegas for the entire month he was there, playing to a packed house every show as thousands more were turned away. No matter where we looked, all we could see was the name ELVIS—

on television, newspapers, banners, and billboards. The King had returned.

Initially, Elvis's triumph in Las Vegas brought a new vitality to our marriage. He seemed a different person. Once again, he felt confident about himself as a performer and he continued to watch his weight and work out every day at karate.

It was also the first time that I felt we were functioning as a team. I made several trips to New York, trying to find unique accessories for him to wear onstage. I bought scarves, jewelry, and a black leather belt with chain links all around it that Bill Belew would later copy for the famous Elvis jumpsuit belts.

I loved seeing him healthy and happy again, and I especially enjoyed our early days in Vegas. The International provided an elegant three-bedroom suite that we turned into our home away from home. During his show I always sat at the same table down front, never tiring of watching him perform. He was spontaneous and one never knew what to expect from him.

On occasion, after his midnight show, we'd catch lounge acts of other performers playing Vegas or we'd gamble until dawn. Other times we'd relax backstage, visiting with entertainers captivated by his performance. This was the first time I'd been with Elvis at a high point in his career.

With the renewed fame came renewed dangers. Offstage he could be guarded by Sonny and Red. Onstage he was a walking target. One night that summer Joe and Sonny were tipped off that a woman in the audience was carrying a gun and had threatened to shoot Elvis. A true professional, Elvis insisted on going on. Additional precautions were taken and everyone was on the alert. Elvis was instructed to stay downstage, making himself a smaller target, and Sonny and Jerry were poised to jump in front of him at the slightest sign of suspicious movement in the audience. Red was positioned in the audience with the FBI agents.

The show seemed to take an eternity. I glanced at Patsy apprehensively and she in turn grasped my hand as we comforted each other, longing for the night to end without incident. Vernon remained backstage, never letting Elvis out of his sight and praying, "Dear God, don't let anything happen to my son."

Because of this and other threats, extra security was arranged wherever Elvis appeared. Entrances through backstages, kitchens, back elevators, and side exits became routine.

Elvis had his own theory about assassinations, based on the murders of the Reverend Martin Luther King, Jr., and Robert F. Kennedy. He felt that the assassins gloated over their "accomplishments," and told his bodyguards that if any attempt were made on his life, they should get the killer—even before the police. He didn't want anyone bragging to the media that they'd killed Elvis Presley.

Sonny and Red lived in so much tension these days that they were constantly frenzied. Suspicious in crowds of overzealous fans, they were quick to respond to any sign of danger. Compared to Sonny's diplomacy, Red's reputation was to act first and ask questions later. Eventually, numerous assault-and-battery charges started piling up against Elvis. When Vernon warned him about Sonny and Red's aggressiveness, Elvis said, "Goddamn, Red. I hired you to keep the sons of bitches away from me, not get me in any legal binds. Somehow you're going to have to control that red-headed temper of yours."

Although Elvis would joke about the death threats—and there would be several more throughout the Vegas commitments—the fear and constant need for security heightened the pressure of nightly performing.

In the beginning when Elvis began doing regular Vegas engagements, we girls visited frequently. We'd fly in over the weekend, sometimes bringing our children, spend three or four days, and then return home.

On the days we were apart I'd take hundreds of Polaroids and home movies of Lisa. She was growing so rapidly I didn't want him to miss out on her development. Daily he'd receive his "care packages," as I'd refer to them, including tape recordings of me teaching Lisa new words and Lisa mimicking me. Each week, upon my arrival, I'd paste photos on the mirrors in his bedroom to remind him that he had a wife and child.

During his first couple of engagements he still seemed humbled by lingering doubts of whether the public was fully accepting him. At this point he had no interest in outside affairs or flirtations, his concentration on daily rehearsals and performances every evening excluding everything else.

Later he would become more cocky. The crowds' admiration took him back to his triumphs in the early fifties and he found it hard to come down to earth after a month of nightly cheers. His name on the International's huge marquee would be replaced by the next superstar. The offices on the third floor would be cleared out and incoming calls for reservations would stop.

Thriving on all the excitement, glamour, and hysteria, he found it difficult to go home and resume his role as father and husband. And for me the impossibility of replacing the crowd's adoration became a real-life nightmare.

At home in Los Angeles, there was just the usual group around—strictly a family atmosphere. This abrupt change was too much for him and soon he developed the habit of lingering in Vegas for days, sometimes weeks, after a show. The boys were finding it increasingly difficult to resolve the conflict between working for Elvis and maintaining a home life.

Crazed with inactivity and boredom, Elvis became edgy and temperamental, a condition exacerbated by the Dexedrine he was again taking to control his weight.

Sometimes, to ease the transition home, Elvis would insist we all pile into cars and head for Palm Springs. Since our marriage we had spent many weekends there sunning and watching football games and late-night television, but after Lisa was born, my needs changed. The Palm Springs heat was too much for her, the long drive boring, the idleness of resort life wearying. One weekend I suggested, "Elvis, why don't just you and the guys go down?"

From that time on, the guys developed their own life-style in our secluded desert home. Occasionally we wives would be invited to spend the weekend, but by and large, Elvis now considered Palm Springs his private refuge.

He made it clear that this time away was good for him, giving him a chance to think, to hang out with the guys. In reality Elvis was lost. He did not know what to do with himself after Vegas. He escaped in more powerful, unnecessary prescribed drugs to raise his spirits and ward off boredom.

After he had conquered Vegas, it was agreed that Elvis should go back on the road. Colonel immediately began booking concert tours around the nation, starting with an impressive run of six sold-out shows in the Houston Astrodome, which earned over one million dollars in three nights.

The night I arrived in Texas to watch the performance, Joanie, Judy, and I flew in on a private jet. I looked down on the Astrodome and found it hard to believe my eyes. The length of a football field—and already sold out. It made *me* nervous. I could imagine how Elvis felt.

Elvis too found the Astrodome overwhelming. "Goddamn," he said when he first walked in. "They expect me to sell this son of a bitch out? It's a goddamn ocean."

However dwarfed he was by the giant facility, he electrified his audience. Houston was our first run-in with mass hysteria. The limousine was strategically parked by the stage door for Elvis's immediate getaway. Even so, screaming fans surrounded the car, frantically yelling out his name, presenting flowers, and trying to touch him.

If anything, Houston was an even greater victory than Vegas. The King of Rock and Roll was back on top. The strain of sustaining such a hype was just beginning and, for the moment, I could believe that everything would still be all right. I did not realize the extent to which Elvis's touring was going to separate us, that this in fact was the beginning of the end. After Houston Elvis began crossing the country, making one-night stands, flying by day, trying to catch some sleep to maintain the high energy level demanded by his performances. From 1971 on, he toured more than any other artist—three weeks at a time with no days off and two shows on Saturdays and Sundays.

I missed him. We talked constantly of being together more, but he knew that if he let me join him, he couldn't refuse the requests from regulars whose marriages were also feeling the strain of long separations. For a while a group of us would fly in from time to time, but this didn't last long. Elvis noticed that his employees were lax in discharging their duties to him when spouses were present, and he established a new policy: No wives on the road.

I didn't really miss the one-night stands, a tedious routine at best: Jump off the plane, rush to the hotel, unpack as little as possible, since you had to check out the next day, go to the performance, then back to the hotel for a little rest before heading back to the airport. Everything was the same except for the name of the town.

It was the day Elvis suggested I come to Vegas less often that I became really upset and suspicious. He'd decided that we wives would attend opening and closing nights only.

I knew then I'd have to fight for our relationship or accept the fact that we were now gradually going to grow apart as so many couples in show business do. As a couple, we'd never sat down to plan out a future. Elvis, individually, was stretching as an artist, but as man and wife we needed a common reality.

The chances of our marriage surviving were slim indeed as long as he continued to live apart from Lisa and me, and in bachelor quarters at that. It came down to how much longer I could stand the separation. Elvis wanted to have his cake and eat it too. And now, as the tours and long engagements took him even further from his family, I realized that we might never reach my dreams of togetherness. I had trouble believing that Elvis was always faithful, and the more he kept us apart, the more my suspicions grew.

Now when we went to Vegas, I felt more comfortable at the openings. He was always preoccupied with the show and I felt he needed me then. On closing nights I always felt uneasy. Too many days had gone by, enough time for suspicions to poison my thoughts. The Vegas maître d's invariably planted a bevy of beauties in the front rows for the entertainer to play to. Curious, I would scan their faces while watching Elvis closely to see if he seemed to direct his songs to any girl in particular. Suspicious of everyone, my heart ached—but we were never able to talk about it. It was to be accepted as part of the job.

Backstage one night Vernon was jokingly negotiating

for a key that had been tossed to Elvis. She was an attractive middle-aged blonde—Vernon's type. Elvis said, "Daddy, you've got enough problems at home with one blonde. You certainly don't need two."

"Well, okay," Vernon said. "You're going to have problems of your own if your wife goes out in the street looking like that." I had begun wearing skimpy knit dresses and see-through fabrics that were daringly revealing. Lamar and Charlie whistled and gave wolfcalls, while Elvis proudly showed me off.

The jokes I played on him were also efforts to get his attention. One night, after he'd left early for a show, I put on a black dress with a black hood and an exceptionally low-cut back. When it came time for Elvis to give away kisses to the girls in the audience—a regular part of his show—I went up to the stage. Instead of kissing me, he kept on singing his song, leaving me to stand there. With my hair hiding the dress strap around my neck, I appeared from the back to be nude from the waist up. I could hear the "oooh"s and "ahhhh"s of the audience. They were under the impression that a topless girl had cornered Elvis and that he couldn't figure out what to do.

I kept whispering to him, "Kiss me, kiss me, so I can sit down," but he decided to turn the joke on me, and made me wait in the spotlight for the duration of the song. Planting a big kiss on my lips, he surprisingly introduced me to the audience. I felt a bit embarrassed and made my way back to my seat.

Later in the show he'd strut back and forth onstage, tease his audience, talk to them, tell them stories, even confide in them. "You know," he'd say, "some people in this town get a little greedy. I know you folks save a long time to come and hear me sing. I just want you to know, as far as I'm concerned, there won't be any exorbitant raise in price when you come back. I'm here to entertain you and that's all I care about."

Elvis was having an ongoing love affair with his audience and the next time I was home alone I knew I had no choice but to start more of a life of my own.

It was with that thought in mind that Joanie, my sister Michelle, and I planned a short trip to Palm Springs. In the course of the weekend I opened the mailbox to check the mail and found a number of letters from girls who had obviously been to the house, one in particular signed "Lizard Tongue." My immediate response was disbelief, followed by outrage. I dialed Vegas and demanded that Joe find Elvis and bring him to the telephone. When Joe said Elvis was sleeping, I told him about the letters and insisted I speak to Elvis. Joe promised that he would have Elvis call as soon as he woke up. He did, but it was clear that Joe had filled him in on the situation and Elvis had his explanation ready. He was totally innocent, the girls were just fans, they were out of their minds if they said they'd ever come to the house, and besides, it was their word against his. As usual, in the end I apologized for putting him on the spot, but things at this point were becoming too obvious.

He said, "Get out and do things while I'm gone, because if you don't, you're going to start getting depressed."

Although my choices were limited—he still objected to my taking a job or enrolling in classes at college—I continued my dancing and started taking private art instruction.

Elvis was a born entertainer and although he tried to avoid crowds, disliked restaurants, and complained he "couldn't get out like a normal person," this life-style suited him. He handpicked the people he wanted to be around him—to work with and travel with—and they adjusted to his routine and his hours and his temperament. It was a pretty close clan throughout the years. A few arguments erupted and a few couples left over some misunderstandings, but they usually returned in a week or two.

My view of life had been fashioned by Elvis. I had entered his world as a young girl and he had provided absolute security. He distrusted any outside influences, which he saw as a threat to the relationship, fearing they would destroy his creation, his ideal. He could never have foreseen what was happening as the consequence of his prolonged absences from home. A major period in my growth was beginning. I still feared our separations but felt that our love had no boundaries, that I was his and if he wanted me to change, I would. For years nothing had existed in my world but him, and now that he was gone for long stretches of time, the inevitable happened. I was creating a life of my own, starting to achieve a sense of security in myself, and discovering there was a whole world outside our marriage.

Over the years of playing Vegas, other pressures began to mount. There were more death threats and lawsuits, including alleged paternity suits and assault-and-battery charges. Jealous husbands claimed they'd seen Elvis flirting with their wives, and others continued to charge that Sonny and Red were manhandling them. Elvis began to get bored with these nuisances as well as with the sameness of the show. Inevitably, he tried to change the format, but then he felt it just didn't have the same pacing as the original. He'd add a few songs here and there but then revert to the original. Pointed suggestions that he make changes before the next Vegas date added to the pressure.

Bored and restless, he increased his dependence on chemicals. He thought speed helped him escape from destructive thinking, when in reality it gave him false confidence and unnatural aggressiveness. He started losing perspective on himself and others. To me he became increasingly unreachable.

37

I HAD JUST walked into the living room where I found Elvis and Vernon arguing about Colonel Parker. "Goddamn, Daddy, call and tell him we're through. Tear up the goddamn contracts and I'll pay him whatever percentage we owe him."

"Listen, Son. Are you sure you want to do this?"

"Goddamn right I am. I hate what I'm doing and I'm goddamn bored."

Elvis stomped out the front door, never returning that evening nor the following few. We were mystified. For the first time he was traveling alone—without even one bodyguard. Elvis didn't even know his own phone number; nor did he carry cash. How was he going to get around? Arrangements had always been made for him.

According to Jerry Schilling, Elvis caught a commercial plane to Washington, D.C., with the intention of meeting President Nixon. When he arrived he had a sudden reaction to penicillin he had taken for a bad cold and decided to fly to L.A. He called during a stopover in Dallas, asking Jerry to meet him at LAX with a doctor. He wanted treatments for the reaction. Elvis rested two days in Los Angeles and then continued his journey back to Washington, D.C., along with Jerry and a five-hundred-dollar check that Jerry arranged to have cashed.

During the flight Elvis befriended a young soldier just returning from Vietnam. The soldier must have told him his life story. Before the plane landed Elvis asked Jerry for the five hundred dollars and handed it over to the young man, wishing him good luck. Jerry said, "Elvis, that's all we have." Elvis responded with, "Yeah, but he needs it worse than I do, Schilling."

Later in the flight, he asked the stewardess for a pen and some paper. Elvis was never much of a letter writer, but he now wrote President Nixon a letter explaining how he could assist the youth of today in getting off drugs. It was an impassioned plea, mistakes hastily scratched out and corrected as he poured out his thoughts.

Jerry arranged for a limo to pick them up at the airport and drive them to the White House. It was 6:30 A.M. and Elvis was dressed in black, including his black cape, sunglasses, his large gold International belt, and a cane. He approached the gate looking, as Jerry put it, like Dracula. His face was a bit swollen, and Jerry feared that his appearance would arouse suspicion.

As soon as Elvis explained who he was and that he had

a message for the President, he was promised the letter would be given to President Nixon by nine that morning. Elvis then had Jerry arrange for him to see John Finlator, Deputy Narcotics Director in Washington. Elvis truly wanted to help kids get off street drugs. Another purpose of Elvis's trip was to try to acquire a Federal Narcotics badge for himself.

Elvis was an avid badge collector. He had detective, police, and sheriff badges from all over the nation and the narc badge represented some kind of ultimate power to him. In Elvis's mind that badge would give him the right to carry any prescribed drug he had on his person. The badge would also give Elvis and his Memphis Mafia the right to carry arms. With the Federal Narcotics badge he could legally enter any country both wearing guns and carrying any drugs he wished.

His obsession with obtaining this badge was triggered by a private eye named John O'Grady whom Elvis had hired to handle a paternity suit. O'Grady showed Elvis his Federal Narc badge, and Elvis's mind started clicking immediately: How could he get one himself? John O'Grady mentioned that John Finlator was the man Elvis should see.

Elvis told Jerry to wait at the hotel in case the President called while Elvis himself went to see Finlator. Within an hour, Jerry received a call from Elvis, saying that his request had been denied by Finlator. Jerry was surprised at Elvis's emotional state. He sounded near tears when he said, "He won't let me have the badge." Jerry was able to lift his spirits by telling him he'd just received a call from the White House. "The President read your letter and wants to see you in twenty minutes."

Walking into the White House was no easy feat, even for Elvis Presley. The guards were friendly but cautious as they checked him out. Jerry too was searched before entering the Oval Office along with Sonny West, whom Jerry had called to join them. Sonny had been mystified by the call and was awestruck when he realized he was about to meet the President of the United States.

Elvis was led separately into the Oval Office. Jerry and Sonny were told they had to wait outside, though there was some slight chance they'd meet the President later. According to Jerry, they were brought into the Oval Office in less than a minute. Jerry knew that if there was a way to get them in, Elvis would do it, and he had come through. Not even the President was immune to his charm.

When Jerry and Sonny entered they saw that Elvis had made himself right at home. He introduced everyone and encouraged the President to give Jerry and Sonny cuff links, and was not shy in asking for mementos to take home to their wives. By the time he left the Oval Office he had added this most important badge to his collection. He emerged smiling, a different Elvis from the one who a few hours before was emotionally upset. Nixon overruled Finlator's decision and had the badge sent to the Oval Office, where he could present it to Elvis.

The argument about Colonel that started this escapade was never mentioned again.

38

OUR MARRIAGE WAS now part-time. He wanted freedom to come and go as he pleased—and he did. When he was home, he was attentive and loving as father and husband. But it was clearly understood that I was mainly responsible for the parenting of Lisa.

An incident occurred which made me realize that I needed to spend more time with Lisa. She, Elvis, and I were about to sit for a family portrait. I was dressing her while her nurse combed her hair. Then, as I started for the set, Lisa refused to go with me. "What's the matter?" I asked. "Come on, honey."

"No, no," she kept saying, hanging on to her nurse. When she started to cry, I got nervous and short-tempered, taking her by the hand and urging, as if a child could decipher my logic, "But you've *got* to be happy! You're going to take pictures with Mommy and Daddy."

Each shot was an effort as we tried to coax her to laugh. For a moment we would be successful but then tears would reappear. She even cried sitting on her daddy's lap as I bribed her with toys and little dolls to get a smile.

That's when it hit me. My God, she's so attached to the nurse that she doesn't want to leave her. Now I knew I had to find more time to be with her. She had been affected by my own predicament. Busy centering my life around Elvis, even during his absences, I had neglected not only my needs but my daughter's as well.

I was torn between the two of them. When he was home I wanted to be with him, without other responsibilities, but I also wanted to be with Lisa, knowing how much she needed me.

I began taking Lisa to parks, afternoon parties, and daily swimming lessons at the YWCA, and I convinced myself that soon I'd no longer have to fake it with toys and lollipops and ice cream cones to get her to smile at me.

She would sit between Elvis and me at the dinner table, squeezing spinach through her hands and smearing it on her face. Elvis tried to convince himself that he found all this adorable, but the fact of the matter was that he was finicky about his food. With a good-natured laugh he would excuse himself, telling the maid, "We'll be eating in the den. Lisa will join us after she's finished playing with her meal."

When Elvis was away from home, which unfortunately was most of the time in those days, I continued to dispatch my regular care packages full of pictures and home movies documenting every inch of Lisa's growth. When he was with us, I encouraged him to participate in Easter-egg hunts and other outings, inviting Joe, Joanie, their children, and other family friends to join us.

Lisa and I visited him in Vegas for her birthdays, having huge parties in the suite, where she received everything from slot machines to two Saint Bernard puppies (a gift of Colonel Parker's) to an entire room filled with balloons—everything, in short, a two- or three-year-old shouldn't have and couldn't appreciate.

It was important to me that Elvis be home for Mother's Day and Father's Day, but he'd invariably call and say he couldn't make it, then try to compensate by bringing home extravagant gifts like a marble jewel box filled with diamond rings, necklaces, and earrings, or a whole wardrobe of handpicked designer clothes from a boutique in Vegas. But that wasn't the point. I didn't want the furs and jewels—I had all I could possibly use—I just wanted him home. It was a constant effort, single-handedly trying to keep up family traditions.

Although Elvis much preferred to spoil Lisa, he did discipline her from time to time. Once he paddled her for writing all over a beautiful velvet couch with crayons. Then he immediately went into a panic, wanting me to assure him that he'd done the right thing and that Lisa wouldn't hold it against him. When I told him, "If you hadn't spanked her, I'd have," he felt better. The only other time he touched her in anger was after we'd repeatedly warned her not to go near the pool and she did.

(She remembers this well and is proudly pleased by her two paddlings.)

By the time Lisa was four, she realized she could manipulate the help. Whenever one of them refused to do something for her, she'd threaten, "I'm gonna tell my daddy and you're going to get fired." Since none of them wanted her going to Elvis, they'd let her get her way, from staying up until all hours and skipping nightly baths to staying home from school. The result was that Lisa had trouble learning what was right and wrong and what she could and couldn't do.

"You don't treat people that way," I told her. "It's abusive. Yes, they work for your father. But you don't go around threatening them." Used to seeing people jump at her father's command, Lisa took years to overcome this habit. At family gatherings today with Jerry Schilling, Joe Esposito, and Dee Presley's sons Ricky and David, we still joke about Lisa's imperious past.

Since Elvis had started performing again, our home on Hillcrest had become so public that we could scarcely get in and out of the drive. Photographers actually concealed themselves in our backyard, making their presence known at the most inopportune moments. Once, we were relaxing at the pool, sunbathing, when I leaned over and gave Elvis a lingering kiss. He whispered, "What's that noise? Shhh, be quiet. Sonny! Jerry! It's a goddamn camera clicking off!" Elvis jumped up and they all headed after the poor man, Elvis leading, shouting obscenities and threats. This was one member of the press who I'm sure never returned.

In our three years on Hillcrest, we'd gradually outgrown the house. Lisa and her nurse shared one room, Charlie had the other, and Patsy and Gee and their new baby occupied the cottage out back. Elvis felt we needed more room; he wanted Sonny on call and close by. Discussions about a new home took on a new urgency.

When a couple of old regulars, broke and jobless, showed up at our door, Elvis took pity on them and put them up in our living room. I awoke in the early morning to the sound of blaring music and found the two had passed out from drinking Jack Daniel's and Coke. Half-empty glasses were strewn about the room and ashes littered the carpet. I felt my home was being turned into a boarding house.

"They have no respect for anything," I complained to Elvis later that day. "What if they fall asleep with cigarettes in their hands? We'll all go up in flames. How long do you intend for them to stay?" I was making no secret of my disapproval. "I don't want Lisa around this."

"You're right, Honey. Maybe I'll just head out for Palm Springs tonight."

The search for a new home led us to Holmby Hills, an exclusive area of sprawling estates between Bel Air and Beverly Hills. We found a traditional two-story house, well-situated on a hill, surrounded by two acres of well-manicured lawns and orange groves. It was larger than our other Los Angeles homes, with a high fence and forbidding gates to assure our privacy.

I had hoped that this home would redirect his attention to the family and that his weekends away in Palm Springs would now be spent with us. He had his own office, his own den, his own game room, his own theater, a breakfast room for private meals, and a dining room for family and friends. It was my intention to decorate this home exclusively to his liking, with ideas carried over from the Hillcrest house, which had been his favorite.

The house cost around $335,000, a little over the budget that we had in mind. With some persistence on our part, Vernon warily let me hire a professional to help furnish it. This would be the first house I'd decorated from scratch and I found it tremendously exciting—having plans drawn up, choosing color schemes, fabrics, wall coverings, and antiques. I loved hunting for special pieces of furniture: a china cabinet that concealed a television set, old trunks to be used as coffee tables, and antique vases to convert into lamps. I was so excited with the project that I persuaded Elvis not to look at the preliminary stages and to wait until everything was completed. Decorating became my passion. I found the challenge so absorbing that I was able to forget my worries over our relationship. Instead of pondering my loneliness, I was engaged in constructive work that required all the flair, imagination, and organizational ability I could summon.

At this time another fulfilling and liberating force entered my life—karate. It had been Elvis's love and hobby for years, and when I first took it up, it was just another of my efforts to get his attention and approval, as in the past when I'd enrolled in French classes because he liked the language, took flamenco dancing because he was an aficionado, and ballet because he adored dancers' bodies.

He had long admired kung fu expert Ed Parker, whom

he'd met years ago. I began taking private lessons under Ed's guidance three times a week. I soon learned there was much more to this art than violence. It was a philosophy. I became even more involved when Elvis cheered my progress.

On our return to Memphis, he slept throughout the day and I enrolled in another oriental discipline, the Korean art of Tae Kwan Do. I became as obsessive as Elvis in dedicating myself to this art. A mandatory requirement was memorizing forms, katas, and stances in the Korean language as well as learning the history of Tae Kwan Do.

The training was incredibly exacting. Over and over we'd execute the same movement until perfected. Perspiration poured into my eyes and yet, if I wiped it away, it would mean one hundred pushups under the watchful eyes of the entire classroom, a humiliation I did not desire and managed to avoid.

Now I could understand Elvis's enslavement to karate. It was an accomplishment, an achievement of confidence and physical mastery of self. In 1972, while Elvis was performing in Vegas, I met one of the top karate experts in the United States at the time, Mike Stone. On this particular evening he was acting bodyguard to a prominent record producer. After the show they came to visit Elvis backstage. Everyone was more impressed with Stone than with the boisterous tycoon he was protecting. Elvis was complimentary and he, Sonny, and Red had numerous questions. Several years earlier we had watched Stone at a tournament in Hawaii and we'd admired his fighting technique.

Later that evening, up in the Imperial Suite, Elvis encouraged me to train with Mike. "He has that killer quality. Nothing on two legs can beat him. I've been impressed with him since the first time I saw him fight. He's a real badass—I like the cat's style."

Back in Los Angeles I made arrangements with Mike to drive out to his studio later in the week and sit in on one of his classes. It was a long forty-five-minute drive.

Elvis was right. Mike exuded confidence and style, as well as a good deal of personal charm and wit. A deep friendship would develop. Because of the distance, I decided to continue my training with a friend of his, Chuck Norris, who had a studio closer to my home. Mike would sometimes come to Chuck's studio as a guest trainer.

I was emerging from Elvis's closed world, becoming aware of how sheltered my existence had been. Mike and Chuck introduced me to popular Japanese martial-arts films such as the Blind Swordsman series, and with Mike I attended karate tournaments locally and in neighboring counties, taking home movies and still photos of top karate fighters. I wanted to capture their individual styles so I could share them with Elvis, hoping this was something we could enjoy in common. In the end, though, I made a whole new circle of friends with whom I felt accepted for myself. The martial arts gave me such confidence and assurance that I began to experience my feelings and express my emotions as never before. Accustomed to suppressing my anger, I could honestly vent it now without the fear of accusations or explosions. I stopped apologizing for my opinions and laughing at jokes I didn't find amusing. A transformation had begun in which fear and indifference had no place. Along with this new confidence, off came my false eyelashes and heavy makeup, the jewels and flashy clothes. All devices that I'd depended upon for security I now shed.

I was seeing myself for the first time, and it was going to take a while for me to get used to the image. I had a chance to observe marriages outside our immediate circle, where the woman had just as much say as a man in everyday decisions and long-term goals. I was confronted with the harsh realization that living the way I had for so long was very unnatural and detrimental to my well-being. My relationship with Mike had now developed into an affair.

I still loved Elvis greatly, but over the next few months I knew I would have to make a crucial decision regarding my destiny. I knew that I must take control of my life. I could not give up these new insights. There was a whole world out there and I had to find my own place in it.

I wished that there was some way for me to share my experience and growth with Elvis. From my adolescence, he had fashioned me into the instrument of his will. I lovingly yielded to his influence, trying to satisfy his every desire. And now he wasn't here.

Accustomed to living in dark rooms, hardly seeing the sun, depending on chemical aids for sleep and wakefulness, surrounded by bodyguards who distanced us from reality, I yearned for the more ordinary pleasures. I began to appreciate the simple things that I would have liked to share with Elvis and hadn't: walks in the park, a candlelight dinner for two, laughter.

Elvis must have perceived my new restlessness. A couple of months later in Las Vegas, Joanie, Nora Fike, Red's wife Pat, and I were having dinner in the Italian restaurant at the Hilton between Elvis's shows. The maître d' came to the table with a message that Elvis wanted to see me upstairs in the suite. I remember thinking how unusual this was. Elvis rarely went to the suite between shows.

I went upstairs, filled with curiosity, and when I arrived in the suite I found Elvis lying in bed, obviously waiting for me. He grabbed me and forcefully made love to me. It was uncomfortable and unlike any other time he'd ever made love to me before, and he explained, "This is how a real man makes love to his woman." This was not the gentle, understanding man that I grew to love. He was under the influence, and with my personal growth and new realities he had become a stranger to me.

I wept in silence as Elvis got up to dress for the show. In order for our marriage to survive, Elvis would have had to take down all the artificial barriers restricting our life as a couple. There was too much room for doubt, too many unanswered questions for the mind to play upon. It was difficult for him to come to terms with his role as father and husband. And since neither of us had the ability to sit down and squarely face the issues jeopardizing the family, there seemed to be no hope.

What really hurt was that he was not sensitive to me as a woman and his attempt at a reconciliation had come too late; I had taken possession of my life.

That night I didn't close my eyes at all, grieving over

what I had to tell him. This was my one great love. Looking down at him I thought of all the times I'd traced my fingers over his lips, his nose, brushed my fingers through his hair, always while he slept. And now, I waited for him to wake up, waited for the right moment, if there ever could be one. At this point in our marriage we were so seldom together that I was having difficulty envisaging his reaction to my news; it had seemed so much easier to play it out in my imagination.

It was shortly after 2 P.M. I had already gotten up and started packing my things when Elvis awoke fairly alert and asked, "Where are you going?"

"I have to go back."

"So soon? It's early. You usually don't go back this early."

"I know," I agreed. "But I have to get back. I have things to do." I hesitated. "But first I have to tell you something." I stopped packing and looked at him. "This is probably the most difficult thing I'm ever going to have to say." I took a long pause, hardly able to get the words out. "I'm leaving."

Elvis sat up and asked. "What do you mean, leaving?"

Never in the entire time of our marriage had I ever suggested walking out on him.

"I mean our marriage."

"Are you out of your mind? You have everything any woman could want. You can't mean that, Sattnin. God-damn," he said, his voice filled with anguish. "I don't believe what I'm hearing. You mean I've been so blind that I didn't know what's going on? I've been so wrapped up I didn't see this coming."

"We're living separate lives."

Finally he asked, "Have I lost you to another man?"

"It's not that you've lost me to another man, you've lost me to a life of my own. I'm finding myself for the first time."

He looked up and stared at me in silence as I stood packing and snapped my suitcase shut. I tried to walk to the door but couldn't stop myself from running back into his arms. We hugged, tears streaming down our faces. "I have to go," I said. "If I stay now I'll never leave." I broke away, grabbed my suitcase, and headed for the door.

"Cilla," Elvis called. I stopped dead in my tracks. "Maybe another time, another place," he said slowly.

"Maybe so," I replied, looking back. "This just isn't the time."

And I walked out the door.

My trip to Memphis was unexpected and brief and there was only one purpose—to get my belongings. I wanted to spend as little time as possible there. Graceland had been my home, and it was difficult saying goodbye to everyone. The staff, most of whom I'd hired, seemed to know without my telling them that I was leaving for good. No one said a word, but their tearful hugs spoke volumes.

I found Dodger in her room—now downstairs—and

sat at her feet as she rocked in her chair. "Oh no," she said, "don't tell me that, Honey. You don't mean it." Then, realizing I did mean it, she hastened to ask, "You're gonna call me, aren't you, and keep in touch?"

"Yes, Dodger. I'll always be there for you. I'll come back and visit. We'll talk just like we always have, and nothing will ever change."

"You're like my own," Dodger said. "It's not going to be the same here without you. Poor little things. I feel so sorry for both of you."

Grandma wept as she tried to understand why two people who love each other should part. "I tried to tell him to spend more time with you—you and that baby."

"It's nobody's fault, Grandma. It's just life. We still love each other. We always will."

"I believe you'll get back together again, Hon." She was wringing her hands. "God knows, you two young'uns love each other enough."

There was a view of green pastures beyond Grandma's window—Sun, the old barn, and all the memories that went along with the happiest time of our lives. Thank God it was a beautiful day; I always hated rainy days at Graceland—they reminded me of the lonely winters when he was gone.

In the warmth and sunshine outside, I strolled around the grounds, looking one last time at the front porch where Elvis and I had sat on the steps, dreaming of a European trip that would have taken us back to Goethestrasse, where we'd met. Gazing over the lawns and the long circular driveway toward the Music Gates, where the fans always waited, I wondered if I'd ever return. I made my way back between the little craters left over from fireworks wars, and, in the garage, ran my hand over the shiny surface of a go-cart. I couldn't believe it was over.

39

LIKE MOST COUPLES breaking up, we went through a rough period before we finally accepted the fact that we were separating. We were divorced on October 9, 1973. Although Elvis and I had continued to talk regularly, we hadn't seen each other over the past few months, which had been a period of strain and tension as attorneys attempted to work out details. Eventually Elvis and I resolved them ourselves. We were both sensitive enough and still caring enough of each other's feelings to know that we wanted to avoid bitter accusations and futile attempts to assign blame. Our principal concern was Lisa, whose custody we agreed would be mutually shared. We remained so close that Elvis never bothered to pick up his copy of the divorce papers.

Accompanied by my sister Michelle, I waited in the

courthouse in Santa Monica, California, for him to arrive, and when he did, I was shocked by his appearance. His hands and face were swollen and puffy and he was perspiring profusely.

With Vernon and Michelle and our attorneys following, we went into the judge's chambers. Elvis and I sat before the judge and held hands as he put us through the formalities of the divorce proceedings. I hardly heard a word, I was bewildered by Elvis's physical condition and kept running my fingers back and forth across his swollen hands.

I wondered whether Elvis's new girlfriend, Linda Thompson, knew how much love and attention he needed. "Sattnin," I whispered, "is she takin' good care of you—watchin' your weight and your diet, waits for you to fall asleep at night?"

Then the judge was finished. The dream I had had of a perfect union was over. The hope of an ideal marriage, which had consumed all my thoughts and energy since I was fourteen, had ended with the simple stroke of a pen.

Feeling a great sense of emptiness, I walked with Michelle to my car. Elvis, his father, his attorney, and a few of the guys walked over to his limo. In passing I waved, he winked. The affinity we shared for each other would always be there. We continued to talk frequently, particularly about Lisa, who we knew would be unhappy. We wanted her to know that she would not, in any way, be deprived of either of us. When we were together it was as if we'd never parted, exchanging loving kisses and sitting arm in arm with her in our laps, and, when we were apart, we never criticized each other.

She'd visit Elvis often in both L.A. and Memphis. He assured me that he would take good care of her, but his life-style was such that I could not help worrying. I'd call to check on her nearly every night she was away. It was 1 A.M. in Memphis when I asked Elvis, "Did Lisa have her bath, and is she in bed yet?"

"Yeah, she's taken care of," he said. "She's in bed, fast asleep."

Within minutes, Aunt Delta called me and complained that Lisa wasn't in bed and she couldn't get her to take her bath. I talked to Lisa, who said, "Well, Daddy wanted me to stay up."

When I called Elvis back, I said, "I thought you told me she was in bed."

"Ah, let her stay up," he said. "It's no big deal."

Her daddy handed everything over to her on the proverbial silver platter, which created conflict when she'd come home and have to deal with reality. We had a running debate on how she was to be raised. "To hell with values," Elvis would say, joking. I knew that it was essential that Lisa gain some perspective, but try to explain that to Elvis Presley.

As the months passed, Linda Thompson became his constant companion and was good for him, I felt. He began taking trips to Aspen and Hawaii, getting out more, because of Linda's outgoing personality. When we spoke, he seemed to be in good spirits.

His movie career was at a standstill, and he focused on Vegas appearances and touring. Elvis had trouble seeing himself "a forty-year-old man still shaking to 'Hound Dog.'" He had other ambitions. He once talked of producing, even directing, but he never took steps to pursue either.

Then came an offer. Barbra Streisand and Jon Peters approached him to star opposite Barbra in a remake of *A Star Is Born*. When Elvis called me from Vegas, I got the impression he was going to do it. His energy and enthusiasm were electric. It was a film classic and he saw a chance to make a breakthrough into dramatic roles. He was confident he could play Norman Mayne.

"It looks like a sure thing," he said. "Just the details have to be worked out." But the project ran aground on those details. It was Jon Peters's first movie. That he was to direct this film with no credits, no track record, presented a problem in Colonel Parker's estimation. Another difficulty was the fact that Elvis's billing would be second to Barbra's—something the Colonel wouldn't hear of. The project was rejected, leaving Elvis despondent over the lost opportunity.

In time, it became evident that he was letting his health go. His behavior at times was deliberately self-destructive. On a few occasions he'd say, "I'll never make it much beyond forty." We've all made such statements, but with Elvis the thought was deep-seated and chronic. Gladys had died at forty-two and, like Gladys, he wanted to go before his father, sensing that he himself couldn't bear another loss.

From time to time, I'd hear that he had checked into the hospital. Concerned, I'd call, asking, "Are you all right?"

"Sure," he'd say, laughing a little to show me it was all a big joke. "Nungen needs a little rest, Sattnin." Then I realized he'd gone to the hospital for the same reason he had during his Army days. It was his way of taking a little rest; he needed to get out of Graceland and away from all the pressures.

By 1976 everyone was becoming alarmed over his mental state as well as his physical appearance. His face was bloated, his body unnaturally heavy. The more people tried to talk to him about this, the more insistent he became that everything was all right.

The Colonel was even concerned about Elvis's actions while onstage. Elvis started forgetting lyrics and resorting to sheet music. He was acting erratic by ignoring the audience and playing to the band. A few shows were canceled and no one could predict whether or not he'd appear onstage.

In the absence of any significant professional challenge, Elvis created his own real-life dramas. His fascination with guns was now an obsession. He became paranoid over death threats, and from his association with the Memphis local police, he had access to lists of local drug pushers. He felt he personally should get them off the streets. Phoning me late one evening, he said, "Cilla, you have anyone you want taken care of? Strictly top secret."

The style, grace, and pride that for the past eight years had been the hallmark of a Presley live performance now bordered on self-parody. Frustrated with the lack of challenge of each passing show, Elvis resorted to sheer flamboyance, symbolized by his costumes, each more elaborate than the one before, loaded with an overabundance of fake stones, studs, and fringes. There were voluminous capes and cumbersome belts to match. He was performing in garb that added thirty-five pounds to his weight. It was as if he were determined to upstage himself instead of relying on his raw talent.

There were times in his final year that he would be criticized on how he related to his audience. Some people observed that he joked around with his band too much and left his songs unfinished. Once Elvis even complained from the stage about "bad management" at the hotel, citing a certain employee at the Hilton who was being fired. The following day Colonel Parker asked Elvis to stick to his own business—entertaining—and let the hotel handle its help. Vernon tended to take Elvis's side on this as on every issue, but the Colonel had a right to be concerned.

One of the guys actually told Elvis he was beginning to look more like a Liberace act in the hope that Elvis would take the hint and come to his senses and rely on just his talent. But from the beginning Elvis had insisted: "I just want to read positive reviews. I don't want to hear any negativity." As a teenager he'd been shielded by Gladys from criticism. When she'd filled her albums and scrapbooks, she'd used only the favorable clippings. If he hadn't been so sheltered, he might have had a better perspective on his career. At least he'd have been aware of what was being written about him and possibly used some of the comments constructively.

No matter what he did, his fans still cheered him on. They were faithful to him through good performances and bad, and eventually their love was the only real gratification he received. They endorsed everything he did. Maybe as long as he was getting their cheers, he thought he was doing fine. But in fact Colonel Parker was right when he told Elvis that he'd better get himself straightened out or his whole career would go down the drain.

His personal life was not helping the situation. He was seeing Ginger Alden, who was twenty years his junior, and the difference in their ages was becoming more and more of a problem. He'd say, "I'm tired of raising kids. I don't have the patience to go through it all over again." There were conflicts—many. Ginger did not like touring, one-night stands. She was close to her family and didn't want to leave them. Elvis tried bringing half her family with them, but that only created other problems. "She spends more time with her sister and mother than she does with me," he complained.

In discussing his dilemma, I asked, "Do you think you can really live with just one woman?"

"Yes," he answered. "Now more than ever. I know I've done some stupid things, but the stupidest was not realizing what I had until I lost it. I want my family back."

I wondered if there was some way we could make it work. "Maybe it was just too early in life for us, Sattnin," I said. "Maybe one day there will be a time for us."

"Yeah," Elvis laughed. "When I'm seventy and you're sixty. We'll both be so old we'll look really silly, racing around in golf carts."

In April 1977 Elvis fell ill and had to cancel his tour and return home to Graceland. Lisa and I were there visiting Dodger. He called me up to his room. He did not look himself; his face and body were bloated. He was wearing pajamas, which he seemed to prefer these days when at home. He held Cheiro's *Book of Numbers* and told me there was something he wanted me to read. His curiosity for answers had not abated. He was still searching for his purpose in life, still feeling he had not found his calling. If he had found a cause to espouse, whether a drugless society or world peace, he would have had the role he sought in life. His generosity was evidence of this part of his nature—his legendary penchant for giving, even to the countless people he didn't know.

But he never found a crusade to pull him out of his cloistered world, a discipline strong enough to counter his escape into drugs. That night he read to me, searching for answers, just as he had done the year before and the year before that and the years before that.

40

WE BOARDED the *Lisa Marie* around nine o'clock that evening, just my parents, Michelle, Jerry Schilling, Joan Esposito, and a few close friends. At first, I just sat alone, in despair. Then I went to the back of the plane, to Elvis's bedroom. I lay there, unable to believe that Elvis was really dead.

I remembered the jokes Elvis used to make about dying. He'd say, "It'd really take something for me to leave this earth." Yet he wore a chain around his neck that had both a cross and a Star of David on it. He would joke about it, saying he wanted to be covered in all areas, just in case.

He'd had a fear of flying, but he never showed it. Elvis never showed any of his fears. He felt he had a responsibility to make everyone else feel secure. So he gave the impression he was self-assured, because he didn't want to let any of us down.

I thought of a time when we were on a flight home from Los Angeles. There was a lot of turbulence, and the plane was shaking badly. Everyone on board was frightened. Everyone but Elvis. When I looked at him, he was smiling, and then he took my hand. "Don't worry," he said. "We're gonna make it." Suddenly, I felt safe. There was a certainty about Elvis. If he said it was going to be, then it was going to be that way.

The trip seemed endless. By the time we reached Memphis, I was numb. We were ushered into a waiting limousine, to avoid the crush of photographers. Then we sped off to Graceland, where we were met by frantic, disbelieving faces: relatives and close friends, the maids—the same people who had been around us for so many years. I had spent most of my life with these people and seeing them now was devastating.

Most of Elvis's close family—Vernon, Grandma, her daughters, Delta and Nash, and others—congregated in Grandma's room, while his friends, and the guys who worked for him, were mostly gathered in the den. Everyone else seemed to just be walking in and out of the rooms, silent and solemn, glancing around in disbelief.

Lisa was outside on the lawn, with a friend, riding around on the golf cart that her father had given her. At first I was amazed that she was able to play at a time like this, but when I talked to her, I realized that the full impact of what happened hadn't hit her yet. She'd seen the paramedics rushing Elvis away, and he was still at the hospital when I'd arrived, so Lisa was confused.

"Is it true?" she asked. "Is my daddy really gone?"

Again, I was really at a loss for words. She was our child. It was difficult enough for me to believe and confront Elvis's death myself. I just didn't know how to tell her that she would never see her daddy again.

I nodded, then took her into my arms. We hugged and then she ran out and started riding around in her golf cart again. But now I was glad she could play. I knew it was her way of avoiding reality.

The night seemed endless. Several of us sat around the dining room table talking, and it was then that I learned the circumstances of Elvis's death. I was told that Elvis had played racquetball with his cousin, Billy Smith, until four o'clock that morning, while Billy's wife, Jo, and Elvis's girlfriend, Ginger, watched them. Then they all presumably retired for the night. But as Ginger slept, Elvis stayed up to read. He called down to his Aunt Delta for some ice water and said he was having a hard time sleeping.

Elvis was still reading when Ginger woke up at nine o'clock that morning, and then she went back to sleep until about 1 P.M. When she awoke, Elvis was not in bed. She found him lying face down on his bathroom floor.

Ginger called downstairs, and Al Strada and Joe Esposito came running up. After calling the paramedics, Joe gave Elvis mouth-to-mouth resuscitation until they arrived. As the paramedics were leaving to rush Elvis to the hospital, his personal physican, "Dr. Nick," arrived and rode in the ambulance, working on Elvis all the way to Baptist Memorial. There the staff tried for another half an hour to revive Elvis, but it was all futile. He was pronounced dead on arrival of heart failure. Vernon then requested an autopsy. The body was taken to the Memphis Funeral Home to be prepared for viewing in Graceland the following day.

As I sat listening to the events leading up to Elvis's last hours, I became more and more disturbed. There were so many questions. Elvis was seldom left alone for any length of time.

Suddenly I knew I had to be alone. I went upstairs to Elvis's private suite, where we had spent so much of our life together. The rooms were more orderly than I'd expected. Many of his personal belongings were gone; his nightstand was bare of books.

I went into his dressing room and it was as if I could sense his living presence—his own unique scent filled the room. It was an eerie sensation.

From the dining room window I could see thousands of people out on Elvis Presley Boulevard waiting for the hearse that would bring his body back to Graceland. His music filled the air as radio stations throughout the nation paid tribute to the King.

Soon the casket was placed in the entrance hall and opened for viewing. I sat in Grandma's room most of that afternoon as thousands of mourners from all over the world passed by, paying their last respects. Many wept; some men and women even fainted. Others lingered at the casket, refusing to believe it was him. He was truly loved, admired, and respected.

I waited for the right moment for Lisa and me to say goodbye. It was late that evening, and Elvis had already been moved to the living room where the funeral was to be held. It was quiet; everyone had left. Together we stood over him, emotional. "You look so peaceful, Sattnin, so rested. I know you'll find happiness and all the answers there." Then I joked, "Just don't cause any trouble at the Pearly Gates." Lisa took my hand and we placed a sterling silver bracelet depicting a mother and child's clasped hands on his right wrist. "We'll miss you." I knew my life would never be the same.

Colonel came to the funeral wearing his usual baseball hat, shirt, and slacks. He disguised his emotions as best he could. Elvis had been like his own son. From the old school, the Colonel was considered a coldhearted businessman, but in truth he had stayed faithful and loyal to Elvis, even when his career began to slip. This day he asked Vernon to sign a contract extending his position as Elvis's manager. He was already planning ways to keep Elvis's name before the public. He acted quickly, fearful that with Elvis gone, Vernon would be too distraught to handle correctly the many proposals and propositions that would be in the offing. Vernon signed.

At the service, Lisa and I sat with Vernon and his new fiancée, Sandy Miller, Dodger, Delta, Patsy, my parents, Michelle, and the rest of the family. George Hamilton was there. Ann-Margret attended with her husband, Roger Smith. Ann expressed her sympathy so sincerely I felt a genuine bond with her.

J.D. and the Stamps Quartet sang Elvis's favorite gospel songs. Vernon had chosen the preacher, a man who hardly knew Elvis and spoke mostly of his generosity.

Elvis would probably have laughed and told his daddy, "Couldn't you have got a comedian or something?" Elvis would not have wanted us to grieve.

After the service we drove to the cemetery, Lisa and I riding with Vernon and Sandy. It was three miles away and for the whole three miles both sides of the street were lined with mourners, and at the cemetery there were thousands more. The pallbearers—Jerry Schilling, Joe Esposito, George Klein, Lamar Fike, Billy Smith, Charlie Hodge, Dr. Nick, and Gene Smith—carried the casket to the marble mausoleum where Elvis was finally laid to rest. There we held a short ceremony and, one by one, walked to the coffin, kissed or touched it, and spoke a few words of farewell. Shortly after, for security reasons, he was moved to Graceland in the meditation garden, his final resting place.

Before Lisa and I returned to L.A., Vernon called me to his office. He was overwhelmed with grief. Did I know anything that would help him to understand why his son had died? He never fully accepted it, and I believed his pain led to his own death, just as Grandma later never recovered from Vernon's death.

When Lisa and I returned home I was torn, trying to decide what was best for her. Many conflicting stories were coming out in the national publications and I knew these could have a lasting negative effect on her memory of her father. I decided to send her to summer camp. There she could be protected from radio, TV, and newspapers and could be with her many friends, including Debbie and Cindy, Joe and Joanie's children.

By the time she returned, I'd already made plans with

Michelle for a long trip to Europe. Anything to get away from the constant reminders that filled the media.

Elvis's death made me much more aware of my own mortality and that of the people I loved. I realized I'd better start sharing a lot more with the people that I cared about, and every moment that I had with my child or my parents became more precious.

I learned from Elvis, often—sadly—from his mistakes. I learned that having too many people around can sap your energies. I learned the price of trying to make everyone happy. Elvis would bestow gifts on some, making others jealous, often creating rivalries and anxieties within the group. I learned to confront people, and to face issues—two steps Elvis had avoided.

I learned to take charge of my life. Elvis had been so young when he became a star that he was never able to handle the power and money that accompanied his fame. In many ways, he was a victim, destroyed by the very people who catered to his every want and need. He was a victim, too, of his image. His public wanted him to be perfect while the press mercilessly exaggerated his faults. He never had the chance to be human, to grow up to be a mature adult, to experience the world outside his artificial cocoon.

When Elvis Presley died, a little of our own lives was taken from each of us who knew and loved Elvis Presley, who shared in his music, his films, who followed his career. His passion was entertaining his friends and fans. His audience was his true love. And the love Elvis and I shared was a deep and abiding one.

He was, and remains, the greatest influence in my life.

Epilogue

I have spent countless hours recalling moments in my past that are to me somewhat significant, memorable pieces of history. When I first decided to tell this story, I had no idea what a difficult and emotional task it would be. So much has been said and written about Elvis from those who knew him well to those who did not and said they did. I hoped to give a better perception of what he was as a man. Other books have painted a picture rather less than flattering, harboring on weaknesses, eccentricities, violent temper tantrums, perversions, and drug abuse. I wanted to write about love and precious, wonderful moments and ones filled with grief and disappointments, about a man's triumphs and defeats, much of it with a child-woman at his side, feeling and experiencing his pain and joys as if they were one.

I would not be honest if I did not say revealing our life, which was so dearly coveted, has been more than a struggle for me. There were many times I wanted to back out, give up, forget or not deal with this labor of love. Some will find I have left out many important dates, specific facts, and countless stories. I don't think anyone can begin to capture the magic, sensitivity, vulnerability, charm, generosity, and greatness of this man who influenced and contributed so much to our culture through his art and music. I did not intend to accomplish such a feat, just to tell a story. Elvis was a giving soul who touched and gave happiness to millions all over the world and continues to be respected and loved by his peers.

He was a man, a very special man.